50 Ways to *Keep* Your *Lover*

Design the Relationship of
Your Dreams Using the
Intimacy Growth Framework™

ANISSA COOKE

Contents

Foreword

In the world of romance writing, where hearts race, passions ignite, and love stories come to life, each page of each chapter must build on the magic of falling in love. But what does falling in love mean, and after the fall, what happens next? As a *USA TODAY* Bestselling Author of novels, novellas, and short stories that focus on women and their journey to self-discovery, I've always been fascinated by romance and love.

When Anissa first shared her idea about her book, *50 Ways to Keep Your Lover*, I was immediately intrigued. Romance is as unique as each of us. The only limit being those we self-impose. As a writer, I've spent countless hours crafting stories about people who are searching. And, often, that search includes a longing for romantic love.

But what happens next?

In Anissa's book, we are presented with some wonderful possibilities of that "next." Through the voice of Belle Wether, our guide, and storyteller, Anissa has skillfully drawn from her own experiences and a wealth of interviews with individuals who have weathered the storms of life and love together. The result is a collection of wisdom, insights, and heartwarming stories that, hopefully, will bring your romantic imagination to life.

In the world of romance, we often get caught up in the whirlwind of initial attraction, the sweet tension of a first kiss, and the heady rush of new love. But, as time goes by, the true test of a lasting, loving relationship is in the moments that follow. It's about building a life together, facing challenges, and continually rediscovering what made you fall in love in the first place.

I believe that *50 Ways to Keep Your Lover* is a little gem to keep nearby because within its pages it offers practical advice and heartfelt anecdotes that will resonate with anyone who has ever loved or aspired to love. Whether you're in the throes of a new romance or celebrating the milestones of a long-term partnership, this book has something for you.

~Angela Kay Austin
USA TODAY Bestselling Author

Preface

In a world that seems to spin faster every day, where instant grat-ification often takes precedence over enduring commitment, the notion of long-lasting love can sometimes feel like a rare gem, hidden amidst the hustle and bustle of modern life. It's a subject that has perplexed, delighted, and confounded humanity for centuries – the art of keeping love alive.

My name is Anissa Cooke, MBA, a researcher and author, and I'd like to take you on a journey into the heart of relationships, where love is not just a fleeting emotion but a timeless bond. In this book, *50 Ways to Keep Your Lover*, I aim to share with you the wisdom I've gathered from countless conversations with remarkable individuals – mature men and women who have not only weathered the storms of life together but have emerged stronger and more deeply in love.

As I began this quest to understand the secrets of lasting love, I found myself sitting across from people with a combined history of love and companionship spanning centuries – not literally, of course, but in the wealth of experiences and insights they generously shared. These are individuals who have walked the path of love, hand in hand, for decades, and they hold within them the treasure trove of knowl-edge that has eluded many in our fast-paced, throwaway culture.

So, how does one go about keeping a lover for a lifetime in a world where relationships often come with an expiration date? It's a question that's worth exploring, and I'm thrilled to take you on this journey with me. But before we delve into the heart of the matter, I'd like you to meet someone special, our storyteller and guide – Belle Wether.

Belle is a fictional character, but she embodies the collective wisdom, grace, and humor of the many men and women I've had the privilege of speaking with. She's your companion on this voyage, a wise and warm Southern woman with a heart as big as the Mississippi River. Through Belle, I'll share the stories, advice, and insights that have shaped the lives of those who have ventured into the territory of love's longevity.

As we set sail on this journey, you might wonder why I chose to embark on this quest. You see, I've always been fascinated by the intricate dance of human relationships, the way hearts entwine, and the sparks of love ignite. But it wasn't until I began to witness the complexities of modern love, where dating apps promise endless options while simultaneously fostering a culture of disposable connections, that I felt a calling to explore the road less traveled – the path of long-term love.

In my quest to uncover the keys to enduring relationships, I stumbled upon a revelation that's both simple and profound: the mindset required to sustain a long-term relationship is fundamentally different from what's pervasive in popular society today. So many single souls, scarred by past heartaches, enter into relationships with an underlying mantra – "Get the most, give the least." It's a defense mechanism, a shield designed to protect oneself from the pain of being hurt again.

Yet, here lies the paradox of love – the more you guard your heart, the harder it becomes to experience its boundless depths. Love, at its core, is about vulnerability, the willingness to open your heart and let someone in, knowing that you might get hurt but choosing to love wholeheartedly anyway.

It's this very understanding that sets the tone for our journey. We're not here to play games or follow fleeting trends. Instead, we're embarking on a mission to uncover the timeless strategies that have allowed couples to build love stories that span a lifetime.

With Belle Wether as our guide and the wisdom of countless love stories as our compass, let's set sail on a voyage of discovery. Let's learn the *50 Ways to Keep Your Lover* and design the relationship of your dreams – one that's built to withstand the test of time and thrive in the ever-changing landscape of love.

Acknowledgements

I would like to extend my deepest gratitude to the incredible individuals who have supported and inspired me throughout the journey of writing this book. Your unwavering encouragement, love, and belief in my work have been invaluable.

Firstly, a heartfelt thank you to Nidia Taylor, Angela Kay Austin (who graciously wrote the Foreword), Christine Burkette, Angela Alvey-Wimbush, Ishmael Etienne, Robert Stanard, and Elijah Batista. Each of you has played a significant role in my life and in the creation of this book.

I am also deeply thankful to the remarkable individuals who graciously shared their stories, insights, and time during the creation of this book. To my wise friends, former colleagues, supportive family members, and cherished members of my house of worship—your contributions were essential in bringing this project to life. Each of you offered a unique perspective that enriched this work beyond measure.

Your wisdom, candidness, and generosity in sharing personal experiences have helped shape the narrative within these pages. I am profoundly grateful for the conversations and the heartfelt support you provided. The stories you entrusted to me have added depth and authenticity to this book and for that I am forever grateful.

Thank you for your continued belief in my vision and for walking alongside me on this journey.

Introduction

In the realm of love, we often find ourselves in search of a guiding light, a voice of wisdom, a confidante who can steer us through the labyrinth of affection and connection. Love, like life itself, is an ever-evolving journey, filled with both delightful highs and challenging lows. It's a voyage we embark upon with our hearts open, hoping to discover the secrets of lasting, profound, and joyous love.

Allow me to introduce you to Belle Wether, your companion and confidante in this exploration of love's boundless possibilities. Belle is a character conjured from the creative mind of Anissa Cooke, inspired by the wisdom of countless mature men and women who have traversed the winding roads of lasting relationships. Through Belle, we have distilled the essence of their experiences, their laughter, their trials, and their triumphs into a character who will walk alongside you on this journey to deepen your connection with your partner.

As we journey through the pages of this book, you'll find that the foundation of any lasting relationship rests on three pillars: communication, intimacy, and trust. Communication is the bridge that connects two hearts, allowing you to express your desires, fears, and dreams openly. Intimacy, in its many forms, nurtures the bond between partners, creating moments of closeness that go beyond the physical. And trust, the cornerstone of any strong relationship, ensures that you can rely on each other through both the joyful and challenging times. Belle Wether's wisdom is rooted in these principles, guiding you to cultivate a relationship where these elements are constantly nurtured and cherished.

Belle Wether is not your typical expert in love. She doesn't hold a PhD in psychology or write for glossy relationship magazines. Instead, Belle's insights are rooted in the real-life stories of women and men who have walked the path of love for decades. She is the embodiment of the collective wisdom of those who have loved deeply, made mistakes, learned, and laughed through it all.

Picture Belle as your dear friend, your favorite aunt, or even the warm, wise voice of your grandmother, ready to share stories that make you smile, nod in recognition, or perhaps shed a tear or two. As you read through these pages, you'll find Belle's anecdotes sprinkled throughout, adding a touch of humor, context, and a dose of good old-fashioned common sense.

Now, you might wonder why we've chosen to name this book *50 Ways to Keep Your Lover*. Some may say it's a nod to a famous song with a similar title, and indeed, music has often been a source of inspiration when it comes to matters of the heart. But more importantly, the title reflects our belief that love, like life, is a journey of exploration and discovery. It's a journey where we strive to find not just one magical formula, but an ever-growing repertoire of ways to keep the flames of passion, understanding, and affection burning brightly.

Introducing the Intimacy Growth Framework™:

To truly nurture your relationship, Belle and I have developed what we call the Intimacy Growth Framework. This framework is designed to be a practical, flexible guide that helps you integrate both grand gestures and small, meaningful actions into your relationship. It's based on the idea that relationships thrive when partners regularly engage in both significant and simple acts of love and connection.

How It Works:

1. **Monthly Big Gesture:** Once a month, plan and execute a larger, more impactful gesture. This could be a special date, a thoughtful gift, or a surprise trip. The goal is to create memorable, emotionally significant moments that deepen your bond. This concept is inspired by the research of Dr. John Gottman, who emphasizes the importance of creating shared, positive experiences to strengthen relationships (Gottman Institute, 2020).

2. **Weekly Small Gestures:** Every week, focus on smaller, more frequent acts of love. These could include sending a loving text, making your partner's favorite meal, or setting aside time to listen to them without distractions. The idea is to maintain a consistent flow of positive interactions, reinforcing the connection and intimacy between you two. This aligns with the "magic ratio" concept from Dr. Gottman, which suggests that successful relationships have a ratio of five positive interactions to every negative one (Gottman Institute, 2020).

3. **Daily Connection Rituals:** Incorporate daily rituals that promote connection. Whether it's a morning kiss, a quick check-in call during the day, or cuddling before bed, these small moments of connection can have a profound impact over time. Research has shown that daily rituals can significantly enhance relationship satisfaction (Fiese, 2007).

4. **Reflect and Adapt:** Keep a journal to track your progress, noting how each gesture or ritual affects your relationship. Reflect on what works well and what could be adjusted. This approach not only helps you stay mindful of your relationship but also encourages continuous improvement. The idea of tracking progress and reflecting on actions is supported by research on relationship maintenance and mindfulness (Carroll, 2013).

As you embark on this journey, remember that the key to success is consistency and intentionality. The Intimacy Growth Framework is not a rigid set of rules, but a guide to help you build a lasting, loving relationship.

In the chapters that follow, we'll delve into a myriad of experiences, intimate moments, and acts of service that can nurture your relationship. You'll find suggestions that range from the light-hearted to the deeply profound, from the playful to the contemplative. Whether you're seeking to rekindle the spark in a long-term partnership, fortify a budding romance, or simply infuse your relationship with a fresh sense of joy, there's something here for you.

Our journey together will take us through moments of laughter and joy, quiet introspection, and shared adventures. We'll explore ways to create lasting memories, those magical moments that become the foundation of a love story. We'll dive into the world of intimate moments, those cherished times when you and your partner draw closer in understanding and affection. And we'll roll up our sleeves to tackle acts of service, tangible expressions of love that demonstrate your commitment and care.

Before we embark on this voyage, a word of wisdom: communication is the compass that will guide you through these 50 ways. Talk to your partner, listen to their desires and dreams, and together, decide which paths you'd like to explore. Many of the steps in this book require collaboration, a joint effort to nurture your connection.

So, let's begin this journey together. Whether you've been together for years, just started your adventure in love, or are somewhere in between, there are always new ways to discover, new moments to share, and new avenues to explore. Belle Wether and I invite you to open your heart and your mind to the boundless possibilities of love, to discover and create your own 50 ways to keep your lover.

With Belle as your guide and the collective wisdom of generations of mature women and men as your inspiration, let's set sail on a voyage through the seas of love, where every wave, every breeze, and every star in the sky has a story to tell.

Prologue

Well hello there, all you lovelies. Let's talk a bit about love.

How many songs and books and poems have you read or sang along to where the topic is love? I'm sure it's too many to count, if I'm being quite honest. Even in those examples, you have so many people talking about the different ways that love affects them, their partner, or those around them. Heck, some writers are known for their work with love stories or romantic poems that you'd only need to hear their last name to think up a verse they wrote.

Love is all you need. Love is all that I can give to you. Love me, love me, say that you love me. Oh love, never knew what I was missing.

If you didn't sing along to any of the above lyrics, I'd be surprised. Seems like there's a lot of popularity that comes with songs being about love, isn't there? But some of what those songs are describing might not be the type of love that you're looking for. Same with the poems or stories. What we're all looking for, sugar, is a kind of love that can't really be described fully in a book or a song. Sure, those can have aspects of that love. The passion, the need for company, the wish that the person you're pining for feels the same way about you, the list goes ever on. It's when you roll that list up that you get something akin to what love really is.

There's a song that comes to mind when I think about love and it's "50 Ways to Leave Your Lover" by Paul Simon. Of course, the title is misleading, since the song doesn't give you all of those fifty ways. It's referenced that there's got to be so many ways for partners to leave each other when they find love lacking in their relationship. In the song, a couple talks about how their relationship is on the rocks and because of that, there's bound to be a whole lot of reasons for them not to be together anymore.

I'd like to think that, if they took a little bit of time to talk to each other, they'd be able to find at least fifty ways to keep a lover.

That's what this book is all about: finding new and different ways for you and your partner to work on your relationship if you're coming up empty with things to do or try. Some of the steps in this book will have you deepening your relationship through physical means. Some steps ask that you and your partner talk about your pasts and explore how those experiences made you into the people you are today. You'll be cooking, cleaning, dancing, singing, laughing, crying, and a whole lot more, but at the end of it all, you'll hopefully get to know more about each other and have your relationship only grow stronger because of it.

I'm hoping that this book is something that you'll be able to use with your lover in order to bring a bit more spark to your relationship. I'm a proper Southern woman and won't assume anything about the lives that you and your lover are living, but sometimes, it doesn't hurt to try something new. Give a few things a try and see if there's anything that sticks. Who knows, you might just find an activity or action that you and your lover want to make a regular part of your lives. If there isn't anything in here that strikes your fancy or doesn't seem doable, think of ways that you can adjust it to fit your lifestyle. Can't take dance lessons? Check out some of those YouTube videos on how to do some specific dances. Not able to stay outside for long periods of time? Move some activities indoors. Not in a busy city or close to a metro area that has a lot of the activities in this book? Heck, there's things you can do that don't require you to be close to anything!

I will end this prologue with a tip that, regardless of any of the steps you follow in this book, you will be able to get a better idea on what your lover thinks and wants to do. I want you to make sure that, before you try any of these steps, you're talking to your lover. Communication is one of the key ingredients to any successful relationship. Sure, it's not the thing that will solve everything that's wrong or needs a new coat of paint, but it will give you an idea of what you and your partner might be lacking in your relationship. Talk with them first and see how willing they are to try any of the steps or experiences in this book. A lot of the things in this book require you to collaborate with your partner, so take that into consideration.

There might be days that you have where you've wondered if there was more to your relationship with your lover. That you've had doubts about keeping the spark of your love alive because you're not able to come up with grand gestures to show them how much you care about them.

I can say for certain that there's at least fifty ways to help keep your lover and you'd be better off trying a few before thinking it's time to leave.

"Exploring new places together injects spontaneity and excitement into a relationship. It reminds couples of the joys of discovery and the importance of creating shared memories beyond the everyday routine."

~ Michele Weiner-Davis

Section 1: Experiences that Create Memories

Sometimes, the best places to visit for a great time with your lover are closer than you think. You don't have to drive for hours or drive to an exotic destination to have a memorable experience at a beach getaway or a fancy resort; sometimes, some of the best experiences can be found right outside your door...or at least within a few miles. How, I hear you asking.

Sit a spell, sugar and let's talk. You see, this book is more than a collection of ideas; it's a love letter to the notion that love is built on moments, both big and small. It's a gentle nudge to remind you that the greatest treasures are often found right in your own backyard. As we embark on this journey through the art of creating lasting memories, remember that it's not just about the destination. It's about the journey itself, the laughter, the love, and the life you share with your partner. Each page turned is a step closer to a deeper connection, a stronger bond, and a love that stands the test of time.

I invite you to walk with me, to learn with me, and to love with me. I've got a few ideas for staying local in order to plan an eventful date night or day trip with the one that you love. You won't have to break the bank either. What you're looking for is an experience that'll stick with you and that's got nothing to do with cost.

These experiences aren't just about having fun; they're about building trust, improving communication, and deepening your intimacy. Whether it's through a shared laugh or a quiet moment of reflection, these activities are crafted to help you understand each other better, open up about your feelings, and create a bond that grows stronger with each new adventure. So give one of these a try and see how they suit you and your lover.

Chapter 1
Music Under Moonlight

O h, sugar, there's nothing quite as nice as being able to head out of your home without bundling up, especially when night rolls around. As spring turns into summer and the weather grows warmer, your neighborhood or a local community group are going to take advantage of that. What you're gonna want to look for are evenings of outdoor events.

In some places, every night of the season has some sort of event or experience that's shared with the community. There's usually some sort of fireworks display in the middle of summer or a fair or carnival with rides that creak just a little too much when they start moving. Having live music at these types of things are common and there's usually whole nights just dedicated to bands and soloists strutting their stuff on a small outdoor stage. These music nights are the perfect time to take your lover and make an evening out of listening to music under the night sky.

The most work you'll probably need to do is researching when you'd want to have your date night. Sometimes there's websites with all of the information you need, sometimes there won't be. Reach out to members of your neighborhood that are involved with community events and see if you can get a schedule. The next step is to find a mu-sical group that plays music that you and your partner enjoy. There's a trick to this: don't be too picky! If you're in a small neighborhood, you might not have sprawling options of music to choose from. If you want to make it a little more fun to choose, get your partner involved in the choice. Find the band with the funniest name or choose one where you know who the singer is. Trust me when I say that making a choice like that will make the event a nicer experience for you both, since there's a funny little memory connected to it.

Once you and your lover decide on what band to see, all that's left is to go! If allowed, make sure you pack some snacks and maybe a little bit of alcohol (only if you partake, I know it's not for everyone, sugar) to enjoy while you watch the performance. If you want to skip bringing anything and you get hungry, there's bound to be food stalls or food trucks nearby the venue that you can grab a bite at. Then just relax and take a seat to listen to the band. Between songs or if there's a break, let the conversation between you and your lover flow naturally. Maybe you'll find out more about each other's music tastes from a night out or you might discover that you actually like a type of music you didn't think you liked. Or maybe, just maybe, there won't be any big revelations between you and your lover. Sometimes, it's nice to just take some time to enjoy being in the company of someone you love while listening to music under the starry sky.

Chapter 2
Summer Sun Rays

Taking a day to enjoy the summer sun is a great thing to do for both your mind and body. You may not be able to enjoy the summer like you did when you were young and out of school, but having that time to just relax without worrying about work is as healthy as you can get. Let go of that stress and let your mind get a much needed break. I'll bet you anything that your partner also needs that kind of relaxation from time to time too. Look, we all know that it's great when you're busy and you're able to get so much work done, but too much of that leads to burnout and, honey, it's never fun when you get to that point. So taking a few days to enjoy the warm weather and sunshine will do you both good. And what better way to soak in some rays than to take a trip to get some sun by the water?

Now here comes the part where you ask, "Ma'am, I thought you said that these experiences won't break the bank. Do you know how much a vacation home costs to rent these days?" And I'll say right back that I didn't mention anything about this being a beach vacation or about it being multiple days. A day at the beach shouldn't be something that gets you in the red as soon as you plan it. Besides, it may take you a few hours to get to the beach, if you're not living near the ocean to begin with. So this experience can be had at a pool too, not just a beach. Whether you live by the community pool or have a neighbor that'd be willing to share for the day, use whatever body of water you can to just take the day and swim for a bit.

To plan, start the day off early. Check to make sure there aren't any storms in the forecast; that'll put a wrinkle in anyone's plans. If there's too much of a chance for a storm, scratch the day by the water and attempt it another day, but don't let your day go to waste. If you need some ideas for a day in, take a look at the next section for some ideas. If the day looks clear, then you can begin your preparation. The essentials of towels, sunscreen, and a blanket are a must. Check the rules of the pool or beach to make sure if you can bring a meal or snacks with you. If not, see if there's anywhere nearby where you can grab a bite or if there's a stand within the vicinity that serves snacks. Take along something to occupy your time if you won't be swimming, like a book that you promised yourself you'd read, and then get ready to head out.

For those lucky enough to afford it, getting out on the water can be a wonderful way to bond with your partner. Whether it's renting a boat, zipping around on jet skis, or paddling in a kayak, there's something truly special about sharing these experiences together. Feel the breeze in your hair, the sun on your skin, and the thrill of adventure as you explore new waters. I know, not everyone can indulge in these kinds of luxuries, and that's perfectly okay. But if you can swing it, it's a fantastic way to spend a day. Just imagine the two of you laughing as you navigate the waves or find a quiet spot to drift and relax. And if that's out of reach, don't worry—there are plenty of other ways to enjoy each other's company by the water without breaking the bank. But for those who can, these moments can be the kind that you'll look back on and smile about for years to come.

From there, just take the day to do what you want while at the beach or the pool. Work on that tan, get in the water and swim a little, stick your toes in the sand (beach only of course; if you have a sandbox near the pool, that can work as well. Just make sure you wipe your feet off before heading back into the water). Or ignore my suggestions and just do what you want to do. It's your day to enjoy however you please with the one you love. Just promise me that you'll head back home afterward looking a bit tanner and a little less stressed than before you went, okay sugar?

Chapter 3
Celebrate Local Culture

I'll bet that regardless of how long you've lived in your current home, you might not know the history about where you're living. Whether it's a small town, a suburb, or the big city, there's always something new to discover about where you're living. And that opens up the door to some neat experiences you can have with your lover while exploring the place where you live.

Wherever it is that you're living can have a deep connection to a certain group of people or the history behind its founding. Explore that and dive into more of what's happening in your community for certain days of celebration or remembrance. If you're unsure of where to look, start on the internet. Take the time to research what the area you live in is connected to and see if there are any events that celebrate that. Maybe your town was founded by immigrants of a certain country and there are parades or festivals celebrating that culture. Maybe your town had something impactful go down in its history and there's a day or week set aside to remember that day and what it's done for the town. Every city, town, and suburb is different, so my examples might not match what you find.

If your partner is new to the area or hasn't had the chance to experience it for as long as you have, see if there are any events that could take up the day as a fun outing. If your partner is into history, then I'd recommend attending remembrance events or places that hold a legacy for the area. I know it's not ideal, but things may get a bit somber at those kinds of spaces, sugar, and I wouldn't want you to have a day when you and your partner aren't in the right mindset. If something like that is something that you both are up for, check in with yourself and your partner to make sure that you're feeling alright and are okay to continue.

So, let's stick with the more fun options in this case, alright? These events could include parades, picnics or fairs, all day festivals, or even a week that includes events every day of the week. Plan accordingly and take time to take in the culture of where you're living. Enjoy the festivities, whatever they are, but don't be afraid to ask questions about what the celebration is for. You and your partner might be surprised to find out the hidden depths of where you live and learn a bit more about a culture you might not be familiar with. Not only will you get a day of fun and food, but you'll also gain a better understanding of where you live and the people that call it home.

Chapter 4
Show Us Your Moves

Now, I'll say it once and then leave you to it: you don't have to be an expert at dancing to attempt anything for this experience. I know I'm not the most graceful dancer out there, but it is fun to cut a rug with friends and family at a wedding. I'd tell you all about what I ended up doing at my sister's wedding, but with the photos and possibly a videotape still out there, I'll just tell you that I found out I was more flexible than my dress was.

If you are not a dancer at all, well, this may turn you on to the idea. Dancing is a language in itself, but you're talking with your body instead of with your voice. Letting your body move to the rhythm of the music around you, grabbing your partner's hips to have them closer to you as you sway, whoo, it's getting me a little sweaty just thinking about it. I think we'll keep those saucier thoughts in the margins, shall we?

Now, I know that not everyone is up for hitting the dance floor. Maybe you or your partner are a bit too shy, or there could be health concerns that keep you from cutting a rug. But let me tell you, there's still plenty of fun to be had just by people-watching. I remember when I was younger, I'd sit in front of the TV, completely mesmerized by the dancers on *American Bandstand* and *Soul Train*. Watching those folks groove and move was entertainment all by itself! So, if dancing isn't in the cards for you, that's okay. Head out to a dance hall, grab a cozy seat, and enjoy the music and the show. You can even sway a little in your chair or tap your toes to the beat. It's all about soaking in the atmosphere and sharing a moment with your lover. Whether you're on the dance floor or just watching from the sidelines, you'll be making memories together, and that's what really counts.

If you're not a dancer, then taking lessons with your partner is a great alternative. Check out your local dance studios or community halls to see what sorts of styles they have classes for. Ballroom dancing is a bit more formal, but helps give you a good sense of balance and footwork. Salsa is a bit more energetic, having you and your partner constantly twirling and tapping around the floor. Swing dancing really gets you moving, with dips and spins that hearken back to the 50's and 60's. There's so many to choose from, so discuss with your partner if one of the classes sounds interesting.

If you'd rather not take a class, it doesn't mean you aren't able to dance anywhere else. Check out your neighborhood to see if there are any dance halls or clubs close by that you can visit. It's all about what you and your partner prefer, in the end. If flashing lights accompanying your music isn't preferable in a club setting, there are other options you have to explore. Doing a bit of research on where a good place to dance will be worth it when you find the perfect place that you and your lover can enjoy for a fun night out. Don't be afraid to visit these dance spots yourself, just so you can gauge what the atmosphere is like and if it'd be a fun place for you and your lover to have a night out in.

The night you're ready to head out to the club or dance hall, make the most of it! Get dressed in your best, get some makeup on, make sure you look in the mirror and can say 'Damn, I look good' before you head out of the house. Show your lover that you're ready for a night out and that you want to look good when you're out with them. If you're going to a dance hall, you can even coordinate your outfits so that everyone knows you're together. It's just a thought, but one that'd get me 'ooohing' and 'awwwing' if I saw it. Then all that's left is to dance the night away! Remember to stay hydrated and if your feet hurt, that means you're having fun!

Chapter 5
Tighten Up
Your Laces

There's nothing like an afternoon outside to get your body feeling great while you garden, hike, or just walk around your neighborhood. The outdoors are a wonderful place to explore or just lose yourself in what nature has to offer. An experience that you and your lover can enjoy outdoors is taking a hiking or walking trail at a nearby park or national forest. Plan a day to just unplug from day to day life and take a few hours to have an adventure hiking through nature.

Get ready for a hike with the proper supplies and a good pair of shoes. Decide with your partner on a particular trail that you want to take and use that to determine how long it would be until you were able to head back home. This is an experience, depending on how extreme you want it to be, that you'd want to let someone know where you're going and for how long you'll be out there. Sugar, I know I might be more nervous than a long tailed cat in a room full of rocking chairs, but safety and a few 'what ifs' should be paramount if you end up off the trail.

Now, there's always the chance that there isn't a group of hills or mountains nearby that you and your partner can adventure on.

Depending on where you live, there might not be things like hiking trails readily available. Instead, look for walking trails or bike trails as alternatives. Check out your local parks and see if they offer anything like that. If not, who's gonna complain if you just take the day to walk around the park instead?

If walking for a long time is something that you or your partner have a problem with, take the day out at a local park or trailhead to have a picnic. Not everyone is athletically inclined (myself included, sugar), so attempting to have a day where all you're doing is hiking or walking on a trail might not be enjoyable for everyone. Find a different way to connect with nature then, whether it is just taking a visit to a local park and parking yourself on a bench or by making a day out of it by having a picnic. You don't have to be active the entire time to enjoy the outdoors.

Spending the day out and about, regardless of what you're doing outdoors, will definitely get you working up an appetite by the time you get home. Plan something simple for you and your lover to enjoy for dinner, maybe even something that you've prepped ahead of time so that all of the work is done. That'll give you both time to wash off the sweat and grit from the outdoors and eat a good meal.

Or what better way to end a day spent in nature than by cooking a delicious meal together? After you've both freshened up, take some time to reconnect in the kitchen. Whether you're whipping up a simple pasta dish or grilling your favorite cuts of meat, preparing a meal side by side can be a delightful way to unwind and bond. Plus, cooking together can be a wonderful prelude to the evening ahead. For more inspiration on creating a culinary experience with your lover, check out Chapter 22, 'Cooking in the Kitchen,' where we dive deeper into how you can turn meal preparation into a fun and intimate activity.

Chapter 6
Take a Culinary Tour

S ugar, one of my favorite things to do is eat and I can bet that it's one of your favorite things to do too. Food has a way of bringing people together, whether it's heading out on a date with someone at a restaurant or making a dish to bring to a family get together. For a lot of people, including myself, food offers a look into their background and culture.

We live in an age where there's a slew of different restaurants and culinary delights right at our fingertips. To be able to experience food from a completely different country without ever having to leave your city? Sign me up! And get on that with your lover, since I bet they'd be more than happy to share in those different types of food as well. Some cities or towns may have their own restaurant week, which showcases family owned or completely outrageous restaurants and food trucks. See if your city has something similar and make a game plan with you and your lover as to which restaurants you'd want to visit.

Make it exciting by choosing places or cuisines that you've never had before. Of course, make sure that you and your lover are good on what either of you can eat based on your lifestyles, but there should be a plethora of different things for you to choose. If you don't have a restaurant week near you, plan your own with your lover. Find places that you've always wanted to try or new restaurants that have opened in your area. Or try and see if you can make a week of visiting one food truck every day for a meal; whether it's meeting up with your lover during a break at work or taking the night off from cooking to get something.

The goal should be, of course, getting a good meal from a place you've never been to before. You can use this exploration of cuisine to find food that you've never tried before and now enjoy or locate a hidden gem in your neighborhood that you wouldn't have found if you hadn't seen it featured in your city's restaurant week. Use these locations as a way to connect with your lover through the food that you eat, but to also get a better idea of what your individual tastes are. Maybe you'll find a good date night restaurant, cafe, or food truck this way?

Chapter 7

Expand Your Heart and Mind

E xperiencing the arts in your city is a great way to show your appreciation for the talents of those from the past and present. I know that there are some areas where you live that might not have access to a museum or a large gallery that showcases these kinds of artwork. You'll need to do your research to look for any small or specifically catered galleries throughout your city, but it will be worth it to take in a day of checking out the creativity that your area has to offer.

Check out the local museum for a variety of artwork from ages past. From pottery to tapestries to oil paintings to replicas of cave drawings, there's so many different sources of creativity a museum displays. Use the art to learn a bit more about the history behind some of the people who lived in your town. Are some of the pieces from immigrants who moved from a different country and brought their practices with them? Is there Native American art on display to show how much the area has grown and changed over hundreds of years? Take the time to read the information provided by the museum to give context to each piece and help you and your lover connect more with what someone years ago created.

Don't limit yourself to museums and art galleries. Check around for any pop-up displays that are going on. Depending on where you live, there could be an exhibit showcasing a movie, with pieces of the set and costumes on display. If you are near a college, there might be a day where art majors showcase their final pieces of the year and allow the public to see them. Even a theater could be showcasing an anniversary and have a mini museum set up in the lobby that features pictures from performances long past and handmade costumes.

One place that I've found in my town that gives visitors a showcase of what sort of talents live there is on the sides of buildings. Years ago, in order to help brighten up the place, the city commissioned an artist to create a mural on the side of an elementary school. The idea spread to other parts of the town and now you can't even go a block without seeing a colorful display painted on brick or concrete. If your city or town has something similar, create a tour for you and your lover to walk in order to see as many of these murals as possible. The artists will usually leave their name, so you can always visit their online gallery to get a better idea of what other kinds of art they do.

Take a look at local craft fairs or farmer's markets. They can host contests for artists who submit work at the beginning of the fair and are voted on by the attendees. There are also auctions where art is sold off to support a charity during the run of a fair or farmer's market. Artists can also set up their own booths and tables to showcase their art, allowing you to purchase prints or original paintings straight from the art maker themselves. Look for the art that can be found in unexpected places and you won't be disappointed.

Chapter 8
All the World's a Stage

A performance is a great way to pass the time and to show your appreciation for the art of theater. Whether it's a professional performance or something that was put on by a local school, it's a great way to see the time and effort that people put into something that lasts only for a few hours on stage. The experience is ephemeral, only lasting for as long as it's being performed and appreciated by those who had the chance to witness it.

Check out local theaters of playhouses in your town or city. There may be a show that's ongoing that you'll have a chance to get tickets for with your partner. Be forewarned that the selection a playhouse has to offer is dependent on what shows they're performing during their season, so if nothing piques your interest at one place, check for other theaters that have performances that you and your partner would enjoy. Sometimes, certain shows just aren't to everyone's taste. I absolutely adore the classics, like Shakespeare and Wilde, but my husband gets bored with anything other than a musical.

Professional theater is definitely a great experience, but you'll still be able to have a great time if you end up watching a play performed by a local college or high school. The students would be putting a large amount of work into remembering their lines and acting out a play on top of working on their studies, which is probably on par with the amount of work that a professional actor has to juggle. School performances usually have more popular or mainstream plays or musicals that they perform, so if there was a show that you never got to see on Broadway, you might be able to see it now.

Of course, you can't rule out one-day/one-night performances that are available during Renaissance Faire season. These tend to be more classic, consisting of Shakespeare or acts that were common during that time period. Don't think that just because the subject matter is something you studied at length in history and English classes that it won't be an enjoyable time. And, if it ends up not being something you end up enjoying, you can always head out into the fair and spend an hour or two experiencing a Ren Faire with your partner. Besides, sugar, no one can say no to a turkey leg the size of your forearm, not even a man who scoffs at anyone dressed as Shakespeare.

Chapter 9
Laughter Is the Best Medicine

The title says it all; sometimes, all you need is laughter. And while you can enjoy it through the wonderful experience of talking with your lover, sometimes you need a special touch to get the laughter flowing. That's where comedians and sketch comedy shows come in. If your city has a comedy club, check out a few of the acts after having dinner with your lover. Go into the show with an open mind if it's amateur night or wait until some more seasoned comedians are headlining the club. If there are acts that have performed before, check on video sites to see if their type of comedy leaves you in stitches.

If you don't have a comedy club near you, check out the local theaters. Sometimes, they host comedians or nights of sketch comedy as part of their seasons. A night of sketch comedy might be a show you'd be more open to, since it can rely on improv and more situational laughs than a comedian's set of jokes. There are also multiple skits or games that can be played, sometimes leading to audience participation, which you and your lover can volunteer to be a part of. I know how fun shows like 'Who's Line is it Anyway?' look, but getting the chance to be a part of it can definitely bring out some funny stories to tell your friends after the show.

Will every act you go to be funny? I hope so. But sometimes jokes fall flat or get a bit too awkward and you and your lover feel the need to leave the premises. Don't let the rest of the night go to waste. Have a backup plan of a funny movie that you both enjoy to make up for the lost laughs. Turn on a few episodes of a sketch comedy show on the web or on streaming that you and your lover can laugh over when you get home. Get that funny bone tickle in however you need to in order to get some genuine laughs.

Chapter 10
Pitch a Tent Under the Stars

G oing out for a few nights to camp outside with your lover is definitely not for the faint of heart. And sugar, I'm not talking about the wildlife you might find. You'll be in close quarters with your partner after having set up a tent that could be a bit grating on the nerves, if it's something you've never done before. So, maybe find a way to take the hassle out of it?

A camping experience first starts with where you'd want to go. Look for campgrounds near your town or national parks that allow for camping in certain areas. Some campgrounds will provide you with supplies to rent, so if you aren't an avid camper, you don't have to break the bank to look for the perfect tent to pitch. Decide on your location and what days you want to go, being mindful of the weather you may encounter. No one wants to sleep under a rainy sky, especially with a floor that'll have you muddy before you can say 'I think we should have stayed home'.

If you've never been camping before, now's the time to study up! Include your partner in looking up how to properly pitch a tent, if it's best to use a campfire where you'll be staying, and the best way to keep bugs and wildlife away from your camp. Expect the worst when it comes to the weather you could encounter, just so you don't get waterlogged. Bring along plenty of food in a container that's wildlife proof. And don't skimp on sleeping bags because despite it being warm during the day, you don't know how cold it'll be during the night. My point is, hun, just don't go into the experience too blind. If you do, you'll end up with skeeter bites in places you never wanted them to be and that might be the least of your problems.

Now if the full outdoor experience isn't for you, there's always campgrounds that offer cabins for rent. This still gets you away from the city and under the light of the stars, without sacrificing some of the things that you've grown used to in a house. Even with a cabin, you can still take walks through the surrounding areas, have a campfire to toast marshmallows on, and, if you're so inclined, take a turn at fishing at a nearby lake or river.

If you're not close enough to a campground or any of the above sounds like something that might be a bit too much out of your price range, there's nothing that says you can't camp in your own backyard. Pitch a tent outside your home, if you have a yard. Go through the preparations you'd normally take for camping, but just a few feet away from your home. This way, if things do take a turn, you've only got to travel a few feet to get back into comfort. Take the time to enjoy the outdoors while also enjoying the company of your lover without the distractions. Unplug and challenge yourself to not check your phone unless you're setting an alarm. You and your partner can give yourselves more time to just be present and in the moment with each other and not glued to a screen.

Chapter 11
Become Tourists in Your City

So, if you've used the previous experiences at all before reaching this one, I'm sure you've learned a lot more about what your city and the surrounding area has to offer. But what about the things that you already knew were there? Some cities have that one tourist attraction that everyone and their mother travels from the corners of the country to see, whether it's a museum or the house where someone famous lived. The question remains: when was the last time you visited those places yourself?

You and your lover can have a day where you explore your town like a tourist. Go to all of the places that tourists visit, whether it's a monument or a museum with a guided tour. Take everything in with fresh eyes and an open mind. Think about why people like to visit these particular places. If your town or city has a focus on a particular person or event in history, see what makes your city so special to them. Learn your history through the lens of someone visiting your town or city for the first time and appreciate that you live in a place that has so much to offer the people who travel there. Who knows, you might learn something new about where you live.

At the end of the day, find a restaurant that's been featured in magazines or food blogs as a must-experience tourist stop. If you've been there before, try ordering something that you and your lover have never tried. If you've never been there before, ask the waitstaff about what dish the restaurant is known for. Be the judge yourself to see if the restaurant or cafe is truly worth traveling out to visit. It may become a new favorite spot for you and your partner when you're unsure of where to go out to eat.

As the day winds down, that doesn't mean that your tourist experience needs to end. Depending on the season and what you're close to, there might be night tours of famous battlefields that claim ghosts walk amongst the grass. Some walking trails also hold night walks and there are museum experiences you can have after normal closing hours. Act like a tourist and take advantage of those events! Sure, some of them can seem cheesy and are specifically made for tourists in mind, but don't let that ruin the experience for you.

Now, this might be an experience that will put a dent in your pocket in terms of where you decide to visit. If you want to make this experience the best it can be, then save up to have it. Places will jack up prices if they know that they're bound to still get people coming in. Still, don't put yourself into a hole if you can't have the tourist experience. There are a majority of national parks and areas owned by them that are free to enter. Some small museums based out of famous houses get their revenue through souvenirs and don't require a fee to enter and take a tour. What I'm saying, sugar, is that you've got options, so use them!

Chapter 12
Shiatsu or Deep Tissue?

If there's one thing that everyone needs, it's time to relax and unwind. The world today has all of this focus on hitting the grind and working nonstop, but that's all well and good until you start to burn out. It's always a good idea to listen to your body and what it needs if you start feeling like that, so make sure you're aware of what you need before it's too late. The question is, what do you do when you feel like you need a tune-up for your body? A massage is the answer!

Massages are some of the most relaxing things that can help your body feel rejuvenated. The aches of weeks of hunching over a desk or the soreness in your limbs after unloading boxes can be massaged out of you and get your muscles feeling normal again. And I'm not talking about that sore you get after a good workout or an accomplished day on the job, I'm talking about that nearly bone deep ache you get when you're feeling out of sorts and considering calling off of work. Trust me, sugar, I know both those feelings all too well.

Couples massages can be something you and your lover can look into. There are spas or massage parlors that even give discounts if you're coming in with your partner. Find one that's close to your home so you won't have to travel too far. Again, you don't want to break the bank for your experience, but expect to spend a bit because of the service you're getting. Also, talk to your partner about what sort of massage you'd want to get. There are all sorts of massages, ranging from hot stone, aromatherapy, deep tissue, shiatsu, and Swedish. See what the parlor you have nearby offers and decide with your partner as to which one you'd want to try.

Plan your day around the massage, since you'll want to make sure you don't do anything stressful afterward to get rid of all that hard work the masseuse put into taking care of you. Let the relaxation that the massage gives you take the time to sink in. After your massage, maybe take the rest of the day to stay in and do nothing. The next section has some good experiences you can have while at home, so you can use the tips there to have a stress free day to completely relax and give you and your partner's minds and bodies the rest they deserve.

Chapter 13
Root for the Home Team

Regardless of what kind, attending a sporting event is an experience best spent with people you're close to. Even if you're not a fan of sports, being surrounded by the people you love who are having a great time can get you caught up in the energy that a sporting event brings. There's something about the energy at a sporting event that can draw you in and get you excited, even if you have no idea how the sport is played.

As long as the event is open to the public, you and your partner can attend it. It doesn't matter if it's a little league baseball game at a park near your house or a pro football game at a stadium an hour away, there will be some sort of game that you and your partner will be able to attend. The question remains: which sport do you choose? That I'll leave for you and your partner to mull over, I can't determine which sport you'd like best or if you have a favorite sport. Pick something that you both would enjoy and, if you can't decide, see if there's a way for you to attend both of the games you and your lover have in mind. Especially if it's a game that's happening in your neighborhood, the ticket prices will be much lower than at a large stadium.

No matter what game you choose to attend, make the most of it. Take a trip to the concession stand to get some food to enjoy during the game. If you're unfamiliar with the sport or who's playing, choose a team with your partner to root for. Or, if you want to make it interesting, have you and your partner root for different teams. Make a bet on who'll get the most points and come up with a low stakes prize for whoever wins. Even if the game doesn't turn out as exciting as you thought it would, you'll still be with your partner and can talk to them in between innings (or periods, or quarters...there's a lot of different time-telling for sports, right?).

After the game is over, see if there are any souvenir stands that you can get a keepsake from. If the game wasn't something you and your partner enjoyed, try and find a silly hat or foam finger you can bring home with you. Make light of it; not all experiences turn out perfect. And, if you've got some time before the day is done, why not check out a few of my other suggestions for a night in?

Chapter 14
Cheers to Us

I 'll admit that, when the mood arises, I'll take a nip of something alcoholic as a way to wind down for the day or if I'm having a fancier than usual meal. There's also something about trying out a fancy bottle of wine or a new IPA to learn more about what you like and don't like about alcohol. Everyone's got their own unique tastes. If you and your partner enjoy exploring new flavors together, it can be a delightful way to deepen your connection.

Check out a local winery, distillery or brewery for any tasting events that they have. For vineyards, this usually includes a walkthrough of the facilities to show just where the wine comes from and what sorts of grapes they have. Vineyard tours are usually done during the late summer and early fall, since the grapes will be ripe and offer a lovely sight as you walk through the rows. With the tours usually comes a tasting, so you'll have the chance to sample some of the vineyard's best with your lover and a few others. There are usually small cheese boards or appetizers that are paired with the tastings, so you and your lover will get some food out of the tour as well. Take your time and enjoy the scenery as you get a little tipsy.

Distilleries are another excellent option for couples looking to explore new flavors together. Many distilleries offer guided tours that take you through the entire process of making spirits like whiskey, gin, or rum. You'll get to see the copper stills up close, learn about the different ingredients used, and discover the aging process that gives each spirit its unique character. Some distilleries even let you sample straight from the barrel, giving you a taste of how the spirit changes over time. After the tour, you can usually enjoy a tasting of the distillery's offerings, often paired with small bites to enhance the flavors. Whether you're sipping on a smooth bourbon or a spicy gin, it's a fun and educational experience that you and your partner can enjoy together.

One of the most memorable experiences my husband and I had was during our visit to the Uncle Nearest Distillery in Tennessee. We decided to take the tour on a whim, and it turned out to be one of the best decisions we've made. As we walked through the beautiful grounds, we were captivated by the rich history of Nearest Green, the first African American master distiller. The story behind each bottle of whiskey was as smooth and full-bodied as the product itself. When it came time for the tasting, I discovered a newfound appreciation for whiskey. I left with a bottle in hand and a new favorite spirit, one that we now enjoy on special evenings together.

Breweries sometimes offer tours of their facilities, but most of the time will have restaurants or stores connected to them that will make it easier for people to sample what they have. If you want to spend your afternoon at a brewery, go after you've already been out with your partner, just so that you're not expecting the experience to take up an hour or two before eating. Brewery food can be a bit pricier than your normal mom and pop diner, but that doesn't mean that they're skimping on anything. Ask your waiter or waitress what pairs best with specific brews that they have on tap. Plan a night out with your lover at the local brewery to try out some interesting flavors to pair with one-of-a-kind beer.

Best practice to make sure that you both have a great time is to set up either a rideshare or a friend to take you to and from the location. Don't let safety slip by when you're going someplace with alcohol.

Chapter 15
Do-Re-Mi

G oing out to a local restaurant or bar might be one of the defi-
nitions of a normal date night, but you know that you can do
a little bit more to make it a night that you and your partner won't
forget. We've gone over live music, comedy shows, and getting to know
your city's roots. Why not visit a place that has a karaoke night in order
for you and your lover to sing the night away?

Now, I know what you're going to say. "Ma'am, I don't know
about you, but I can't sing worth a lick." And that's fine! If you're
comfortable singing, get up onto that mike and belt out one of your
favorite songs. Maybe get your lover to pick one that they know you
love or they like to hear you sing. Or take the opportunity to serenade
your partner to a song that means a lot to them. If you're not someone
who sings, but your lover is, encourage them to try a song or two. Or,
if both of you are more comfortable singing if the other is up there
with you, try a duet.

I promise that you and your lover won't be the worst singers up on
stage. If you're at a bar, there's sure to be someone tipsy who thinks
they can be the next Celine Dion. Pick something that you know
you're going to nail or find a song that the both of you can sing. If
you're nervous, try to find a song that you and your partner know well.
Maybe it's the song that the two of you sing to each other because it's
the only one you know the words to. Or maybe it's a song that was

playing when you first met. Or it could be a song that's connected with a silly memory. Have fun up on stage and relish the applause you get afterward.

The very last thing I want you to do is feel uncomfortable when you're up there singing. So, if you're not eager to get on stage or your partner isn't, don't push yourself or them! Your main goal is to have fun and enjoy yourself while you and your lover are out and about. Pressuring each other to do something you'd rather not do isn't a great way to spend a night out. Sometimes, just listening to other people singing is a fun time. There are plenty of other activities I've got up my sleeve that you and your lover can do instead, so don't try and limit yourself.

Chapter 16
Painting Is Silent Poetry

S omething that's grown in popularity over the course of the last few years are those group painting courses. With a wine glass in hand and a leader guiding you, the entire group creates a piece of art that, regardless of skill level, looks identical to what the leader has displayed. There are usually different themed nights at a studio that have you and your fellow classmates painting different pictures to match with that theme.

Talk with your partner about taking one of those courses. Choose a painting that the two of you would want to have displayed in your home. Or find a night where there's a couples theme, allowing you to make and take home two different paintings that make up one complete scene. In the end, it's up to what you and your lover would want to do, but keep yourselves open to what sort of paintings you'd want to have displayed.

There are bound to be studios close to home that host these classes, so check out the stores or head online to research. They'll provide you with a sample of what you'll be painting, along with what time the classes are. Since the classes involve some sort of alcohol to drink while you're painting, the times are usually set in the evening after a regular 9 to 5 workday. There might also be special classes held over the weekends, depending on the studio, so if you're not sure how to start or end your weekend, this is another option for you.

So, onto the painting. Regardless of whether or not you're an expert or artistic, these paint nights are specifically tailored to be easy to follow. Having an instructor walk you through the steps and showing you how to create the art they want you to work on will help to keep your focus and make sure that you're understanding what to do. Don't be afraid to ask for help from your partner or help them out if they're struggling. Work together in order to make your artwork the best it can be.

At the end of the night, if you and your partner both imbibed on some wine or other alcohol, get a ride home from a friend or a rideshare service. When you've sobered up, take a look at what you created and find a place to hang them. If your pieces match, see if there are two separate rooms you want to put them in or have them be a part of a matching wall set. If they're something you're proud of and you had a very memorable night, consider having them framed. They'll be reminders of the fun you had with your lover and can be great conversation pieces whenever you're entertaining friends or family.

Chapter 17
Unchained Melody

S omething that doesn't seem to be as common as a painting studio with classes is a pottery studio. There might be some specialty shops that offer kilning and clay you can purchase or have already fired pieces that can be bought and glazed. It's the kind of thing that would be very popular, but not many places have studios. Whether it's because of how long the process takes, pottery is a craft that many have tried but few have mastered.

Pottery is very hands on, whether you're creating your own piece or painting something to be kilned. It is a process, one that would make a great weekend project for you and your lover to be a part of. Check for any studios nearby and take a look at what they have to offer. Know that this process also takes a lot of patience and attention to detail, so if you or your lover would get frustrated about how long it'd take for you to shape a cup without it toppling in on itself, maybe find another activity. This book is to help you keep your lover, not argue over how much water you'd need to shape your clay.

Some studios offer classes on how to shape and create different pottery pieces. Others offer time slots where you're able to use their equipment freely, for a price. I'd recommend the classes as a start, especially if you're new to pottery and don't know how to work clay. As you get more confident or if you have a background in crafting that has you and your lover familiar with clay, then take the time to visit a studio to create your own pieces.

Now this might be something you need to look up for context, but I'm sure that you've seen references or an actual scene involving pottery where a man is sitting behind a woman, helping her shape what's on the wheel. This scene played out in the movie *Ghost* (which I highly recommend; Patrick Swayze was a heartthrob) as something very intimate between the two main characters. Have you and your lover reenact the scene yourselves (being mindful to not disturb other people in the studio or class). Sure, you'll probably get messy and the thing you're trying to make might not come out perfect, but if you do end up getting your creation kilned, you can look at it with memories of a fun time.

Chapter 18
I Pick You

Now, this activity might be something you'll need to head outside of town for, depending on where you live. As much as I'd love to think everyone's got a farm nearby, there's a lot of cities out there. But, I digress, you'll need to find a farm that has one or more activities that are open to the public. Check for farms that have orchards or pumpkin patches for your best bet, but there might be a few that have fields full of flowers as well. The main draw should be a 'pick your own' theme, regardless of what it is.

Head out to a farm and spend the day picking your own apples, strawberries, flowers, pumpkins, or whatever your local farm has to offer. Make sure you plan for a nice day that's sunny and comfortable, regardless of the season. Take the time to explore the fields you're picking from, walking and talking with your lover as you look for the best things to choose to take with you. This might be a great time to learn about what sorts of fruits they prefer or what color flowers they like the most. Use what you learn to deepen your understanding of your lover and share your own thoughts so that you both get to know a bit more about each other.

If you're picking fruit, ask a member of the farm what to look for in order to get the sweetest berries or the best pumpkins for carving. For anything edible, see if there's a specific dish that the farm recommends you try with what you gather. Get information on how best to keep the flowers you picked fresh. Take this chance to learn about what the area has to offer. Ask about what the farm has to offer in other seasons, just in case you and your lover are looking to return on another day. Who knows, you may have found a spot that the two of you visit every year as part of a tradition.

After your day at the farm, make sure you use what you gathered. For the flowers, display them prominently and make sure they stay fresh as long as possible. Looking at them for as long as you're able to will help keep the memories of your time at the farm fresh. If possible, see if there are seeds you can harvest from the flowers so that you're able to plant some in your home or garden.

For your fruits, make a special dish out of what you picked out. Don't limit yourself to desserts; I know I'm one to think of tarts or pies whenever there's fresh fruit involved, but you can do so much more! Maybe try to make a jam out of any berries you got. Add apples and peaches as part of a dinner dish to create a sweet balance to a savory meal. Pumpkin seeds can be roasted for a snack while you're carving out a jack-o-lantern. Enjoy the fruits of your labor as a tasty treat to cap off a lovely day.

Chapter 19

Pack Your Bags and Hit the Road

A gain, yes, I know that this section is for keeping yourself and your lover close to home, but read on! I promise I won't steer you wrong. You can have a mini vacation away from home without straying too far from home. The goal here is to take a little time for yourself and your lover, without having to drive hours to get there.

Plan a small getaway on a weekend that you and your lover have free. Find a nearby city that's maybe a one or two hour drive away from your place and book a hotel room for a night or two. Then, pack your bags and head out. Sure, you're not going anywhere that's completely off the map, but you'll be able to spend a little extra time with your lover without having to worry about the mundane. No chores to do, no meals to prep, nowhere to be except wherever the two of you want to be.

Make the most out of your time away from home. Enjoy what the hotel you're staying in has to offer, whether it's by ordering room service or taking a dip in the hotel pool. If you and your partner are up to it, take a visit to the gym to see what it has to offer. Don't rush yourselves or feel like you absolutely have to do something. Enjoy the feeling of not having to worry about the mundane and use this as an opportunity to just be with your lover without any distractions.

Now, that's not to say that you can't make this mini vacation a bit more planned out. If there are things you'd want to do, like visit certain restaurants or check out a local attraction, do them! Work out things that you and your lover would want to do, but give yourselves some leeway. Say, if you're wanting to head out for dinner, maybe choose a spot where you won't need a reservation. Or take the time to walk from the hotel to your destinations during the weekend, taking your time and exploring the area on foot.

You just don't want to get too carried away and not take the time to relax with your lover. The weekend you spend with them should be free of worry and responsibilities. Leave all of your cares and thoughts of work at home; you can pick those up when you get back from your vacation.

Chapter 20
Rhythm of the Night

S ugar, I love a good concert, but I feel like, in recent years, some of my favorite bands have been harder to see. Ticket prices have gone up and, as much as I love some of my favorite bands, I'm not going to take out a loan in order to get a seat at a stadium to watch them perform. For some of my favorite bands, they're not touring around the world anymore. But that doesn't mean I won't ever get the chance to see them.

For some older bands or solo acts, stadiums aren't the places to see them anymore. Instead, they perform at smaller venues or theaters. Find one of these performers that you and your lover enjoy listening to and grab some tickets to see them live. Sure, it won't be in a huge arena or even outdoors, but you're going to have a blast nonetheless. Take the time to check out the venue before booking seats, just to make sure that you're getting the best experience for what you're spending. Then, all that's left to do is head out and watch the show.

The band that you go see might have a sentimental link to your or your partner's past. Maybe it's one of their songs that you two remember hearing when you first met. Maybe they were a group that you ended up bonding over when you went on your first date. Whatever the reason that connects you both to the singer or band you're seeing, let those feelings be at the forefront when you're watching the performance.

After the performance, whether it's when you're waiting for the venue to clear out enough so you can leave or on the ride home, talk about what those songs mean to you. Maybe reminisce on how much time has gone by in your own relationship and how the band or singer makes you think of your lover. Use this experience to build an even stronger sentimental bond with the band by saving your tickets in a scrapbook or album that you'll be able to look back on for years to come.

"In a world full of distractions, the greatest act of love is to give someone your undivided attention. Quality time is about creating a space where you can be fully present with your partner, where you can listen, share, and simply enjoy each other's company. This is where the magic of a relationship truly happens."

~ **Leo Buscaglia**

Section 2: Intimate Moments that Bond You Together

L et's face it, there are some days where either bad weather or just general feelings of 'I don't want to do anything today' can make the thought of going out anywhere unappealing. Having those days doesn't mean you have to just sit around and wallow in boredom, especially when it comes to having the same mindset as your lover.

Staying at home only offers a limited amount of things to do, but that doesn't mean that you and your lover can't have fun. In fact, these opportunities to stay inside can help strengthen your relationship, believe it or not. I am here to tell you that the walls of your home bear witness to the stories of your love, and the intimacy you cultivate within them can be a powerful force in fortifying your relationship.

You see, the word "intimate" carries a weight of meaning that extends far beyond the confines of the physical realm. Intimacy, in its purest form, is about emotional closeness, vulnerability, and a deep connection that transcends words. It's about two souls intertwining in a dance of understanding, compassion, and shared experiences.

As we embark on this section together, remember that intimacy is a garden – it requires tending, nurturing, and patience. Within the comfort of your own home, you and your lover have the opportunity to strengthen your communication, deepen your intimacy, and build the trust that serves as the foundation of your relationship.

Forget about going out tonight and get cozy with your lover right at home with these ideas. Whether it's a quiet night of cooking together, a movie marathon, or simply enjoying each other's company, these moments offer a chance to connect on a deeper level, creating memories that will last a lifetime. The simplicity of staying in can open doors to conversations that might not happen otherwise, allowing you to learn more about each other and grow closer as a couple.

Chapter 21
Netflix and Chill

B efore we start, I know that not everyone has a streaming service in their household. It's common, yes, but some people don't prefer it next to regular television or just owning a DVD player. This particular experience is about just you, your lover, and a movie or show that you both enjoy. And yes, the connotations of 'Netflix and Chill' can bring to mind some other activities, but I'm a polite Southern woman and will leave those activities to your imagination.

Movie nights are a low stress way to have a good time indoors. There's no wrong way to have a movie night; you can plan it to the nines with a themed night or just pop some popcorn and get comfortable on the couch. As long as it's something that both you and your partner enjoy, then it's all fair game. You can choose a bunch of movies to watch back to back or use the time to finish up a show that you both were watching. Again, it's all up to you as to how you want the night to go down.

The type of movie you watch will set the mood. If you're looking to get in on some 'Netflix and Chill', then pick something that's more romantic and steamy. Pick a comedy if you're looking to laugh after a long week of work or an action flick that'll keep your eyes glued to the screen. Of course, you could use a horror movie as an excuse to stay close to your lover and cuddle with them so neither of you get scared. Either way, make sure it's one that you and your partner agree on. No one ever had a good movie night when they were forced to watch something they didn't want to.

Snacks are a must with a movie night, especially snacks that are nice and portable and don't have you getting up from the couch every couple of minutes to replenish. You could get a large bowl filled with popcorn to tide you over or make a little 'buffet' of snacks in smaller bowls that you can pick from throughout the film. You can work with what you've got available at home or take a trip to the store to stock up, but make sure you get enough for the night.

When it's time to watch the movie, make sure that you've got everything in the same room as where you'll be watching the movie. This makes sure that you've got everything you need and don't need to pause the movie several times to run and grab something from the kitchen. Prep some warm blankets to snuggle up in with your lover on whatever seating arrangement you have, get your snacks into bowls, and, finally, take a seat and watch your movie.

Chapter 22
Cooking in the Kitchen

A night in means that you can either order out for food or make your own dinner. While getting take-out of some of your favorite foods is a great time saver, a home cooked meal definitely has its own kind of charm. Sure, there's a bit more to clean up at the end of the preparation, but the reward is something that's tasty and probably more nourishing than regular take-away.

Why not use cooking as a way to bring you and your partner closer? You can plan a meal with them that you both enjoy, or you can use this opportunity to try out something different. Don't start the process with just cooking; begin with planning. Work out what you want to make with your partner. See if there's any particular cuisine both of you have wanted to eat. There may be a recipe from your past that becomes an option, so don't limit yourself to one specific thing. The possibilities are endless when it comes to cooking, so long as you've got the right ingredients for it.

Once you've decided on your meal, you've got the chance to work together with your lover to create it. Use the prep time to catch up on your day and, as you talk, help each other out with the dicing, tenderizing, or juicing that comes with the recipe. The focus on the recipe can bring a certain amount of casualness to the conversation. Let it flow naturally as you get into the more intensive cooking or baking part of your meal. Some recipes can require a bit more time for cooking, so use that time to focus more on your lover.

Now, cooking together can be more than just a practical task—it can be an opportunity to turn up the heat in your relationship. As you prepare your ingredients, take a moment to savor the sensory experience together. The scent of fresh herbs, the texture of ripe vegetables, and the rich aroma of spices can all serve as delightful preludes to your meal. Why not have a little fun with it? As you chop, stir, and season, you might find playful ways to incorporate some of the ingredients into a bit of flirtation. A sprinkle of salt here, a dash of spice there, and suddenly the kitchen becomes the perfect setting for some culinary seduction.

For example, feed each other a taste of what you're cooking or maybe sneak a little kiss between steps. You might even find that some ingredients—like strawberries, chocolate, or even whipped cream—lend themselves particularly well to adding a touch of romance to your evening. Remember, it's not just about the meal you're preparing; it's about enjoying each other's company in a way that brings you closer together. After all, the best kind of cooking is the kind that fills both your stomachs and your hearts.

If creating a meal from you or your lover's childhoods, use it to learn more about each other. Was this a dish that was passed down from other family members or just a meal that brought back a specific memory? If it's a meal that you've never had before, learn about why you or your lover chose it. Is the meal something reminiscent of a country you've wanted to visit or is it something your lover had always wanted to cook, but never had the chance to do so? This'll help you get a better sense of how you and your lover think, along with giving you things to remember for future date nights. You'll thank me later when you remember your lover likes a specific kind of food and you've forgotten to cook something.

Finally, after finishing your cooking, it's time to eat! Dig in with your lover over candlelight or a movie, but make sure that you're both eating together. It's important that you're sharing the experience with your lover, even if they've got a few things to say about your cooking. Your dish may end up being a meal that you'd happily cook again or something that you're satisfied about trying once. No shame in that, but now you've got a nice memory to look back on that you and your lover shared together.

Chapter 23
Literary Lovers

I'll be the first to tell you that variety is the spice of life. There's a lot of good in the tried and true, the safe and familiar. The go-to sometimes is the best option you have, but if you're not at least trying other things, then what you're doing ends up too predictable or, even worse, stale. That goes for meal planning, date ideas, and, especially, in the bedroom.

Now, I'm a proper Southern woman who won't ask about what you and your lover get up to in the bedroom, but I know that there's nothing better than the normal, the expected, when you're there. After a long day of work or just a day of frustration, knowing that the usual lovin' that your partner can give you is a comforting thought. And when you're experiencing it, that comfort only they can provide is something special. That doesn't mean you have to stop with the old and completely switch over to the new; just be open to try a few new things. Or read about them.

When you and your partner are in the mood for something a bit different in the bedroom, try erotic literature. This can be a book that you or your lover have already read and want to share the steamy scenes or it could be a book about different experiences you can have in the bedroom. Look through it together or read through separately and convene in the bedroom to share your opinions and if there's anything specific either of you want to try. Either way, these books can at least give you some ideas for ways to shake things up.

If your book is more about positions and experiences, pick a night during the week to try out a few things (preferably when you have off the next day; from experience, no one wants to go into work with a pulled muscle from getting a little too frisky). See if there's anything that you and your partner really enjoy or absolutely hate. Have fun with it; testing the waters with a certain position may get you or your partner to realize that, with some tweaking, it could work for the both of you. Take the time to experiment and learn what you both enjoy from the differences and similarities to what's in the book.

Reading an erotic book that has a full storyline and characters might not seem to be an activity that you and your partner can share in together, but hear me out! Take turns borrowing the book to read, using two bookmarks to make sure you don't lose your progress. Take the book to work and read a few pages while you're having lunch or when you're winding down for the night afterward. The steamy scenes might give you some ideas for the bedroom and even provide a few roleplay opportunities for you and your lover to act out.

Look at me over here, blushing up a storm. Let me give you a few more PG options next, okay, sugar?

Chapter 24
Walk Down Memory Lane

I t's no secret that knowledge is power, so it's good to know about your partner as you deepen your relationship with them. You've gotten to know them when you first started your relationship, so you'll need to keep up that communication as you continue. Through conversations and experiences you share with them, you can learn more about what they enjoy and what makes them tick. Of course, there's lots of other ways to find out what your lover is like, but let's focus on what they were like long before they met you.

If possible, take a trip with your partner to their hometown. See if you're able to visit the home they grew up in. Getting to walk around the place where your partner grew up, seeing remnants of their past, is a way to get a conversation going about what it was like for them growing up there. Be open with your partner and understand that there might be things they don't want to talk about. Listen to their explanations without judgment and take that knowledge to heart. You don't need to comment on what they're explaining or if they start to get wistful, just listening will show that you're there to support them and are using this opportunity to learn more about them.

It may not be possible to visit your lover's former home, but that doesn't mean you can't visit other places. Take a walk around the neighborhood where they grew up. Have your lover describe the changes that have occurred or haven't occurred since they last visited. If there was a place that your partner liked to visit often when they were a child, see if you can visit there. It could be anything from a park to a mall to a place of worship.

Ask your partner what makes that place special to them or if it brings back certain memories for them. Chime in with a few memories of your own, if you both frequented similar places. Use those shared experiences as a way to bring you closer and to learn more about how your pasts have shaped you into the people that you are today.

Yes, there might be moments where you'll need to take a break or leave because of something a bit too painful for your partner to voice, but keep that knowledge in your heart. Understand how precious it is that your partner, at the very least, trusted you with a reaction to their pain. Trust like that is a precious thing, sugar, and keeping that trust will make sure that the two of you continue on the path to a healthy and wonderful relationship.

Chapter 25
Let's Get Physical

Exercise isn't always the most fun thing to do. Especially if it's something that you've worked into your routine, it can sometimes feel like a chore to complete. Just another checkmark to put on a list of things to do for the day and then, once it's done, you just move on to the next thing. If you're doing it as a way to get into shape and are just beginning your workout journey, it's even harder to get a routine together that is both challenging and something you're fine with doing multiple times a week.

Spice up your routine by inviting your partner to exercise with you. If you both exercise at different times, make a plan to have a joint workout together at a time that works best for the both of you. You and your partner may already know about the goals you're looking to meet with your exercise, but if you don't know, share them with your lover. Maybe you're both looking to lose some weight or work on building up muscles. Maybe you both have different ideas of what an exercise routine can do for you. Either way, know what each of you are looking to get out of each workout you plan.

Now, you can have this workout in your home or apartment or take it to a gym that the two of you go to. If you're lucky enough to have one nearby, take your workout to a beach or park. Go somewhere that the two of you feel comfortable being, giving yourself some freedom as to where you both want to have the time to exercise. If you or your partner are a little self-conscious, don't force yourself to exercise out in public.

For each workout, know what you and your partner plan to do. This way, you're able to hold each other accountable if you begin to slow down or want to stop. Build each other up during tough exercises, cheer your partner on if they do more reps than they usually do, comfort them if they can only get through one set of a difficult workout. This can be a new way to show your partner what they mean to you and validate them if they're feeling like they're not doing enough.

If there is time and energy after working out, treat yourself and your partner to something relaxing to cool down. Don't just skip to the next task of your day—take the time to enjoy a refreshing post-exercise shower with your partner. Not only will it help wash away the sweat and grime, but it's also an opportunity to reset and relax together. Cleanliness can often open the door to more intimate moments, creating a sense of comfort and closeness that's hard to achieve when you're still sticky from a workout. So, lather up, rinse off, and let the warm water soothe your tired muscles. It's the perfect way to transition from the intensity of exercise to a more tender, shared experience.

Or, if you both are really tired, get dressed in something cozy and turn on a movie or show that you both enjoy. Let your bodies come down from the high of your workout and let yourselves relax before getting on with the rest of your day.

I think the term is called a 'cool down' period, right? Maybe save the more strenuous activities for when you've taken a rest. Just thinking about exercising rather than getting in bed...I don't know about you, but as soon as my head hits the pillow, I'd be done, regardless of what my partner's plans were.

Chapter 26
For Your Viewing Pleasure

S peaking of turning on something to watch, have you seen just how many shows are out there right now? Not even counting the streaming-only fare, there's hundreds of shows that have run their course on television. It's nice to think back to those days where you had to wait a week to find out what happened to your favorite character after an episode ended on a cliffhanger. Oh, I remember those days where you'd run into the kitchen to grab a snack during a commercial break between episodes, only to hear your watching partner yell, "IT'S BACK ON!" Those were the days...don't look too deep into that, I am certainly not giving you a hint on my age.

Now, it's so much easier to find a show and watch multiple episodes in a row so that you're not left guessing. Commercials are a thing of the past and being able to pause and rewatch bits and pieces of an episode without missing anything is a luxury that those who are old enough never had.

Find a show that's a bit more fantastical in nature. Of course, there are hundreds of fantasy shows that cater to a lot of different things.

Are you looking for a dramatic show that's going to keep you guessing after each episode? Do you want something with a bit more romance? How about something comedic? There's so many to choose from, so grab your partner and try to find your new show based on what you're both looking for.

Now, this might seem pretty simple. I mean, sugar, you and your partner are choosing a show to watch together and are probably going to watch it together, right? Well, make sure that the two of you are watching it only when you're together. No skipping ahead if your partner's out of town for a few days, no coming home to see your partner curled up on the couch and a spoiler playing out on the television. Stick to a promise that the two of you will watch the show together and won't watch it while the other isn't there.

This works best when it's a show that's already completed or nearing completion. This way, you're able to work out with your partner how many episodes you'd want to get through a day and schedule a time to watch the show to its end. You'll be able to better schedule around any days that you or your partner won't be around and give yourselves enough time if plans do come up.

Whatever you do, never, and I mean NEVER, watch an episode without your partner present. If you plan to watch something together, stick to it, even if it's tempting. I'll tell you, the cold shoulder I gave my husband when he watched not one but two whole episodes of one of our favorite shows without me had him freeze up quicker than an ice cube in the Arctic.

Chapter 27
Aloha

I think one of the things we take for granted from our partners and lovers is casual displays of affection. The quick brush of fingers against your own, the peck on the cheek they give you before heading off to another room of the house, resting their hand on your back while you show them something, these are just a few of the things your lover may do to show that they're comfortable with you and want to express their love for you. For some, your lover might not be someone who's had those tiny displays of affection given to them, so they might be hesitant or unable to perform them on you.

Meet them with some affection of your own. Try this: every time you or your partner head out for an errand or come back from work, greet them with a hug and a kiss every time. Even if they were gone for a few minutes, giving them physical affection will show that you're happy to see them, regardless of how short their excursion was. If your partner isn't one for a lot of kissing and hugging, try something else. Your display of affection can be a shoulder squeeze or a hair ruffle.

Before doing this, make sure you communicate with your partner as to what you're doing and work with them on what they're most comfortable with. Everyone's got different love languages, so understand that, maybe, touch isn't the best way to greet your partner. Workshop other ideas on how to show them appreciation when they come home. Maybe you can give them a flower or small handmade chotchkies they can collect and store. Accumulating those small things over time will be a true visual representation of how much you missed them on their travels.

Don't force a specific type of affection on them if they're not comfortable or if they come into the house not in the mood. There are so many other ways of showing that you care for them, you don't have to limit yourself or think that there's not much else you can do. Work with your partner on how best to handle those rougher days and what would help them feel loved and appreciated when they get home. At the end of the day, one of the best things you're able to do is communicate with your partner on how yours and their needs match up.

Chapter 28
Say Cheese

Sugar, it's definitely a new age when it comes to making memories. There's so many websites and apps that let you record all sorts of content, file sharing sites make it easier than ever to send out memories to others, and you don't even need to carry an honest to goodness camera around in order to take great photos. Do you remember some of the things people had to do to get pictures developed? Remember those little single use cameras that you could get at any hole in the wall shop in a tourist town? It is good to see that the art of capturing memories hasn't died out, but it definitely has evolved.

Don't be shy about taking pictures of happy moments with you and your lover. If something about the way they look on a certain day or the way the sun hits their face on a day at the beach, take a moment to snap a picture. Take pictures at the parties you attend, of your friends and families having a great time, of your partner's face mid-laugh. Create a virtual or physical photo album with those pictures and pull it out on rainy days or on days where you and your partner need something to help you smile.

The pictures don't have to be perfect or in a certain order. So long as you're taking a few during events or when the mood strikes to commemorate the occasion. Don't stay behind your camera or phone for too long; experiencing the things you're taking pictures of will help those memories stick around longer and you don't want to be rude by not actually taking part. There's so much drama nowadays about people taking too many pictures and not being in the moment with their family or friends, but there's some truth to it, at its core. Click the shutter sparingly, but don't let great opportunities pass you by when all you're doing is taking pictures.

See if your partner would want to take the pictures instead. After all, you are sharing these experiences with them, so they may have different things that they'd want to capture with you as the subject of the photo. Don't be offended if you end up not looking your best in those photos, but let yourself remember how much fun you had at the time. Besides, if your partner's the one who's capturing you through the viewfinder, then you should already know that they thought you looked lovely.

Chapter 29

Hands on Ten and Two

Driving from place to place is probably one of the most common ways people get around nowadays. Nothing really seems too close anymore. I miss the days of being able to walk a few blocks to the general store to get everything you needed in one trip. Now, it's a bit of a process whether you're driving somewhere close by or much farther away.

Longer car rides can get boring once the novelty of car karaoke has worn off. Imagine, you and your partner are headed to a vacation spot or get together and you decide to take a break from singing and talking for a moment. If your partner is the one driving, move your hand to rest on their thigh, giving it a squeeze every now and again. You can do the same thing if you're driving. If you're not driving, you can reach out to rub the back of their head and neck, giving them a mini massage of sorts to help with any stiffness they have from sitting and watching the road for so long.

Don't go too far; the last thing you need is getting too distracted. The small touches and squeezes will make sure to let your partner know that, even if you're not talking, you're present and there with them as you get to your destination. This type of touch is great for your partner if their love language is physical touch. You won't be able to fully hug your partner while you're both in the vehicle, so the touches and squeezes might be able to help them recharge a bit. Also, don't move quickly to immediately touch your partner without warning. You can let them know you want to rest your hand on their neck or their thigh. Just looking out for you and your lover, sugar, don't want them to suddenly swerve.

If you're the one driving, take your time with the touches. Don't do anything too involved that will have you taking your eyes off the road or have both hands removed from the steering wheel. Little touches are fine, but make sure to get your hands back on 10 and 2 when you're finished. If you're getting closer to your destination, maybe begin a few more playful touches (ideal if you've got to stop at a hotel first). Get your partner a little revved up to get out of the car and do something a bit more physical after sitting still for hours on end when you're at your destination.

But again, hun, safety first!! Last thing you need is a story to tell an officer on why you were swerving. And no, being love drunk isn't an excuse.

Chapter 30
A Walk to Remember

We've already talked about exercise and how sharing in that activity with your lover can help the both of you to work towards your individual fitness goals. What we haven't touched on is just how walking around with your partner not only assists with those goals, but also can give you both time to talk and reflect on things going on in your lives. Even if it's just around the block or on the walking trail at a nearby park, walking is a low impact exercise that gets you moving without getting you too winded.

You can take these walks daily or weekly, in the end it's up to you and your partner to decide how you'd want them scheduled. It's best to walk during a time where you and your partner don't have anything pressing scheduled before or after, so early evening may be the best time for one. Head out to your walking spot and then, well, just walk. You can use this time to talk to your partner about their day or walk silently to just enjoy being outside. Take it slow, but keep at a pace that the two of you can comfortably meet.

Being outdoors and walking can do a lot of good for your overall health and wellness. Doing this with your lover can provide you with another activity that you two can share, without the hustle and bustle

ANISSA COOKE

of your lives weighing on you. Use this as a time of reflection and bring up topics that might be weighing on your mind. Being outside while talking about these types of things can make it easier to speak up about them. It also gives you and your partner an out once you reach home and you can both retreat to separate rooms to think about what was said, not having it linger in your home after talking about something heavy.

You might also find a new favorite spot to relax at, if you're walking in a park. Take the time to explore the scenery with your lover, taking a break on a park bench to point out any flowers or animals that are nearby. Depending on the time you go, you may have the place all to yourself, giving your walk a much more intimate feeling than if you were doing it while the park was crowded. This could become a frequent spot for you and your lover to relax in and let the sounds of nature whirl through the open air.

Chapter 31
Compliment
Your Partner

Again, sugar, I know what you're thinking. And I know that this step looks like something I'd come up with if I was running out of ideas. But, in all honesty, when was the last time you truly complimented your partner? Was it something you did automatically because of something they did or the way they looked or did you end up tacking it on to the end of a sentence?

There are times when we all feel insecure with things about ourselves. It doesn't even have to be with looks; you ever have a thought in your head about an experience you had, where, if you'd said something different, it would have made how people view you so much better? Sometimes, our mind likes to revisit those memories that have us hollering into a pillow out of frustration. I'm sure both you and your lover have thoughts that you're not good enough or that you shouldn't be able to have a great relationship because of who you are. It's time to stomp out those thoughts by making sure that you and your partner know that you're loved and cherished.

If you're not one to compliment your lover, start small. If they style their hair in a particularly cute way or wear an outfit that they picked out special, let them know how good they look. If they're the ones who mainly cook meals, compliment their cooking and how much you appreciate them doing that task. If you get home from work to see that your partner cleaned up around the place, compliment them on how they took time out of their day to clean a room or your entire home. It may not seem like these compliments will have an immediate or great effect on your partner, but having them know that you appreciate the things that they do and how they've taken care of themselves will definitely boost their confidence.

As someone who's not shy about complimenting my lover, you might need to get a bit more creative with what you say and how you say it. Don't make it seem like you're trying to please your partner by telling them exactly what they want to hear every single time you're complimenting them. Talk to them about what it is that they're unsure or insecure about. Learn what makes them happiest. Understand what they want to be praised for. This is the perfect opportunity to get a deeper understanding of your lover and how they see the world around them as well as themselves.

After complimenting your partner, take in their reactions. Are they happy with what you're telling them? Are they bashful at being complimented? Gauge their reaction and understand what you'd need to do in order to make them feel more comfortable. If they ask you to stop complimenting them, do it! Not everything is a sure-fire way of getting closer to your lover, so understand that they might not need the affirmations that you want to give to them. Understand if other compliments about certain aspects of how they live or what they do might be better than others. Communicate with your partner to learn what will make them feel their best.

Chapter 32
PDA ASAP

I think something that all of us can agree on is showing your partner affection in public makes a little thrill go through you. You're showing the world that the person you're with is someone you cherish and enjoy giving affection to. Sneaking a little kiss or giving them a hug in public may cement that feeling that your partner is your own, no matter who sees you with them.

For some, PDA might not be a thing you do often. You or your lover might not be the touchy type or your love languages aren't based on physical affection. With this suggestion, I'm only posing the idea that you take a little time to have those types of moments with your lover out in public. The most important thing about this suggestion is that y'all are comfortable with it. I don't want you trying to plant a kiss on your partner's cheek while they're feeling uncomfortable with you doing so.

Talk with your partner about PDA. Is it something they'd like to try or something they want more of? Or is it something that they'd be comfortable with later in your relationship? Use this as a jumping off point to better communicate with your lover about what they are comfortable with and why. If anything, this can be a great way to learn more about what your partner likes and what to avoid in the future, so make sure you listen carefully to what they have to say.

See what sorts of actions they wouldn't mind doing while out in public. Are they alright with holding hands or having you put your arm around their shoulder? Is hugging too much for them? If you're not in constant contact, would they be okay with you brushing their hair out of their face or bumping their shoulder with your own? In the end, it's up to you and your partner as to how you want to proceed. Don't try to force anything that neither of you want; I can promise there's dozens of other ways you can show affection for them out in public.

Chapter 33
Shall We Play a Game?

P lan a game night with your lover to spend a night with something fun to pass a few hours with. Oh, I do love a good board game, that's for certain, but I know my partner can get a little competitive. If you've never played a board game, card game, or video game with your partner, pick something simple and easy in order to gauge how the two of you act as you play. A little competition is all fun and games until it ends in an argument that has the two of you staying in separate rooms for the rest of the night. So, plan accordingly.

There are so many different kinds of games out there that you can play, not all of them being overly competitive. If you and your partner are up to challenging each other and won't get too carried away, settle on one on one games that have you pitted against each other to get a certain amount of points. The rules don't have to be overly complicated; I'd suggest finding something that you and your partner can complete over the course of an hour or two, but has replayability. Trust me, you don't want a game to be something that you spend multiple nights on (looking at a certain monetary game...that's a week of my life I will never get back).

Card games also offer various quick to play games that can be completed over and over again. It's also a lot simpler to play than some board games; sometimes, all you need is a deck of cards. No worrying about losing small pieces or setting up a board just right, just shuffle and deal. Again, I offer the same warning that you'll need to make sure that you and your partner won't have a fight if someone loses.

If you and your partner are looking for a modern twist on game night, consider diving into the world of video games together. Video games can be a fantastic way to bond, offering a blend of cooperation and light-hearted competition. Choose a game that suits both of your interests—whether it's a cozy, cooperative adventure where you work together to achieve a common goal, or a playful rivalry in a head-to-head match. The key is to pick something that encourages teamwork and communication or provides a fun challenge without sparking frustration. As with any game, the focus should be on enjoying each other's company, so steer clear of games that might lead to unnecessary tension. Whether you're exploring virtual worlds together or battling it out in a friendly contest, video games can bring a fresh and exciting dynamic to your quality time.

An alternative to traditional games or video games is doing a puzzle. This is a great way to still pass the time together, but you and your partner are working together towards a goal instead of against each other. There are so many puzzle sites out there that can even have you create your own puzzle out of a photo collage. I think it might be a great surprise to have a puzzle night with your lover, only to put the final piece in and see that it's a collage of some of the memories you've shared with them over the years. Get some glue formulated for cardboard and you've got a wonderful keepsake to mount on your wall.

Chapter 34
Entertain the Besties

I think it's an established fact that you and your lover have a good relationship with each other, but what about your relationship with the other people they spend time with? Does your lover know who your friends are? Have you all ever spoken or gotten together to get to know each other? Maybe it's time to change that.

Plan a night at your place with your friends or your lover's friends. Either prepare a meal or appetizers to serve throughout the night or order out so that food can be served piping hot. You can have a themed night, with the friends bringing movies or games for you all to play or it can just be a night where you all catch up after finally having time in your schedules to unwind. Sometimes, all you need is a group of people in one place to have fun without trying to plan your way through an evening to try and keep them all entertained.

Use this time to get a bit closer with your partner's friends or have your friends get closer to your partner. Maybe you all never had the chance to hang out together and you only spoke about your partner in passing. Use this as a way to get closer to your partner's friends and vice versa. If you had already met their friends and didn't seem to feel a profound connection, use the night to let them get to know you a bit better. If it's your own friends that are visiting, gently get them to strike up a conversation with your lover. Listen to them if they're not as on board with your partner as you are, but let them know that you want them to be more friendly with your partner.

Now, I say this next part with all of the love I have in my heart: don't try and plan a night with both you and your lover's friends at once at the beginning of getting to know them. There could be a bit too many people for your place to entertain and you don't want to have cliques forming because certain friends aren't a fan of another group. If you've been with your lover for a number of years, then you can work something out, but don't get overwhelmed right when you and your partner are beginning your relationship.

Chapter 35
Extended Family

It may seem that you and your lover become the only important people in your life, but there are times that the both of you might need to include other members of your family into your lives. This can include anyone from parents, siblings, or children from another relationship. The most important thing you can do is to be open and polite when you're interacting with these people.

Sure, they might not be the most friendly. One thing to understand when getting into a relationship with someone is that you're not going to get along with everyone in their life. What you can be is supportive, showing that even though you might not be as friendly with members of your lover's family, you're willing to be at events and get-togethers with them without making undo trouble. You see it all the time on the internet where people ask each other if they're in the wrong for not attending events because someone they don't like is there. The reasons can vary, but if it's just because you and that person don't get along, then sucking it up and attending the event without complaining is what you need to do.

The same goes for your partner. I'm sure that in an ideal world, your family and loved ones would be over the moon that you picked someone like your partner to have a relationship with. For those who don't, both parties would need to be mature about the situation. If you see that members of your family are displaying behavior that's not quite right or purposefully excluding your partner from events where other family members' partners are invited, say something. Show your family that you're not going to stand by and let them act like this. Even if you're not speaking directly to your partner about it, this will show that you're supportive of them.

Drama will come out, hun, it's like taxes, always something you've gotta be mindful of and watch out for. Try and work with your families to have outings or parties that include most, if not all, of you and your partner's immediate family. Learn what works and what doesn't, see how people react, and understand that you and your lover are trying to be the bigger people by letting your families into your life.

"Love is not just a feeling; it's an action. When you love someone, you show it through your actions. Acts of service are a powerful way to communicate your love, as they demonstrate your commitment to your partner's well-being. These acts are the foundation upon which strong, healthy relationships are built."

~ **Barbara De Angelis**

Section 3: Acts of Service that Demonstrate Affection

H un, no man or woman is an island. We may make sure that someone is being taken care of while someone else is checking up on you to make sure you're doing alright. When you're with your lover, there's a give and take which comes with that relationship. Communication about this is key; the last thing you want to do is make it feel like your lover is being stifled. If you find your lover doing most of that giving, you'll need ways to reciprocate. Let me help by giving you some ideas to get you started.

As you'll see, these might seem very simple, but putting your own spin on them and using them as a way to show your lover that you care will help to deepen your relationship with them. If there are things on this list that you normally do, try and find something else here that you'd be able to help your lover with. Remember this, my dear: it's not just the action itself but the love and care you infuse into it that makes all the difference. Each gesture, each act, is an opportunity to let your lover know that you cherish them deeply.

And remember, my dear, that every small act of kindness or thoughtfulness is a thread in the tapestry of your relationship. By nurturing these moments, you are weaving a fabric of trust, intimacy, and communication that will withstand the tests of time. The little things you do for each other are the building blocks of a love that is strong, enduring, and fulfilling.

So, as we journey through this section together, remember that these acts aren't mere tasks; they're love's language. They're the tender brushstrokes that paint a masterpiece of devotion, the silent declarations of a love that's as enduring as the slow, winding rivers of the South. Each act of love, no matter how small, strengthens the bond between you and your lover, bringing you closer together and enriching the connection you share.

Chapter 36
A Meal Prepared with Loving Hands

Now, we've talked a bit about how cooking can be something you'd do with your partner as a way to get closer to them. That doesn't mean that a meal made by you alone won't put a smile on their face. I know when my spirits are low, one of the best things that someone can do for me is prepare my favorite dish. It doesn't have to be my favorite; if I make a comment about a hankering for a certain meal, my husband picks up on that and will make sure that he makes it for me.

Learn about what your partner's preferences are for food. Is there something they absolutely won't eat? What's something they could eat for a week and never get tired of? What's a meal that they like to splurge on for special occasions? It's always important to learn about what your partner is or isn't a fan of, especially if they have certain dietary restrictions you'll need to watch out for.

In order to make the meal special, you can choose to make it on a particular day that has meaning to you and your partner, like an anniversary. Don't let that limit you, sugar; sometimes, a regular day can be the best time for a special meal. If your partner had a rough day, offer to cook something special for them. You can use anything from celebrating a promotion or having a sunny day after a week of rain as an excuse to cook up something special for your partner.

Now, the rub comes if you're not confident in the kitchen. Make sure to have a recipe ready and follow it to the letter if it's your first time making a new dish. Set timers, make sure you don't stray too far from the stove, just keep an eye on things to make sure that they're alright. Once it's finished, it's time to serve it up to your partner.

Don't worry if it's not perfect on your first try. Listen to your partner's comments on it and see what you'd be able to do better with next time. I know I had the hardest time making soup because I was too impatient to make a roux to thicken it, but I realized just how important that part of the recipe was. If you're still not feeling confident, have your partner come and help you prepare the next meal. Who knows, you might just learn a thing or two.

Chapter 37
Care for Their Car

Now, I'm not someone who's into automobiles. I like my car, sure, but it's just something that gets me from point 'a' to point 'b' and back again. Still, I make sure I maintain it so that it's able to continue getting me around town without any issues. And maybe I like to see it shine after a nice car wash. My husband, on the other hand, is one of those people that makes sure his truck is spick and span every week. I saw him wax it once, after he cleaned it off from a mud-soaked weekend out camping. I don't get in the way of that, but I know that it's something that is important to him to have maintained.

If your partner has their own car, see if you're able to take it out for the day to get it in tip top shape. Schedule an inspection to make sure that it's running smoothly or if it needs an oil change. If you're taking the car to a dealership for the inspection, they may offer you a complimentary car wash to have it looking nice after they finish. Of course, you'll need to stop by another carwash or service center that can help with cleaning out the interior of the car, so don't worry if the dealership doesn't have it.

Give your partner's car a thorough cleaning, making sure to vacuum around and under the seats and to clear out any hard to reach places that wouldn't get touched in a cursory clean. If you have the time and don't mind waiting before driving the car again, use formulated shampoo to really get the dirt and grime out of the seats. I'm sure that'll at least get the car smelling as fresh as a daisy, even if it's not too dirty. There are also special wipes that can be used on the dash and non fabric parts of the car, so use those to give a special shine to the fixtures. Get some window cleaner to make sure every window is clean and streak free.

If there is something that's troubling about how your partner's car runs or if something needs to be replaced, try and see if you can squeeze in an appointment before your lover needs their car back. It can be as simple as changing out a windshield wiper or as complicated as changing their brake pads, but either way it'll be a welcome relief for your partner that they don't need to worry about something going wrong while they're driving.

Now, whether or not you want to tell your partner what you did to their car is up to you. Maybe you want to surprise them when they hop into it for work and notice that it's looking a bit nicer. Or you can let them know as soon as you get back when they ask where you've been. Regardless of whether or not they're very much into taking care of their car, the fact that you've made sure that your partner doesn't have to worry about getting their car inspected or to have their oil changed will take a load off of their mind. Things like that tend to be something we forget about until it absolutely has to be done, at least in my case. Everyone's different!

Chapter 38
Me Time

Y 'all need to take breaks from time to time. Even if it's just for a day, taking the time to relax and take time for yourself is always a good thing to do. It can help you recharge or just forget about anything stressful for 24 hours. You know when you need that time to relax, but this entry is going to focus on what you can do to make sure that your partner has that time to just let loose.

If you notice that your partner is in need of some 'me time', plan a day where you can take over the responsibilities that they have. Do the chores they normally do, cook for them so that they've got something nice in their stomach, and take care of any important phone calls they might have been putting off. Let them take the day to just lounge around and not feel like they have to be doing something.

If your partner is someone who'd rather be out and about on a day off, then you can give them some cash or a gift card in order for them to go out and spend the day out of the house. You can prepare for this ahead of time by making a 'me time' fund for both you and your partner. Contribute your loose change or spare dollars to it and, when it gets full, see how much you have and use it for a day for yourself or your partner.

Send your partner out to one of their favorite places or get them to have one of their favorite experiences on that day. Book them an appointment at a day spa, get them onto the green for a solo golf outing, or have them go for a shopping trip to get some new clothing. Whatever your partner decides, they'll be headed out on their own. You'll be able to clean your living space, do any chores they'd usually have responsibility over, and do any meal prep that you'd normally do later in the week. Use the time to make sure that when your partner gets home, they won't have to worry about doing anything chore or work-related.

Chapter 39
A Gift that Keeps on Giving

N othing's better than getting a little spoiled every now and again. Of course, if you've been with your partner for some time, chances are you're someone who knows how to give them gifts and experiences that are outside of their usual fare and they know what types of things they can splurge on for you as well. If you're not someone who typically gives extravagant gifts, well sugar, now's the time.

When you hit a special milestone, be it an anniversary or welcoming a new member of the family into your home, solidify that special date with a very special gift. It can be something as simple as a beautiful gemstone necklace, diamond earrings, or diamond cufflinks. I'm not asking you to break the bank, hun, but don't be afraid to splurge a bit on your lover. Of course, make sure that what you're getting is something that they'll actually wear. If your partner isn't one for suits, even at formal events, maybe skip the cufflinks and try for a watch? Or if diamonds aren't something your partner is a fan of, see if they'd want to wear something with their birthstone in it.

You'll want to make sure that whenever your partner is wearing your item, they'll be taken back to the day you gave it to them. That'll strengthen their memory of that day and make it something that they'll continue to remember for years to come. Choose a day where you're having an anniversary of meeting your lover. You can also get them something to commemorate the birth of a child into your family, utilizing the birthstones of you, your lover, and the baby into their gift. Or you could be spontaneous and plan a day of extravagant experiences, ending with you giving them their gift. Don't be shy about asking your partner what they'd prefer, but if you're planning on keeping it a secret, make sure that you're not too blunt about why you're asking, sugar. Sometimes, a surprise is better than the anticipation.

Chapter 40
Sweets to the Sweet

A h hun, sweet tooths are a wonderful thing. Nothing beats a bite of some sugary goodness to get you feeling good and having something sweet in your belly. Everyone's got their own preferences on what they like the most, so either ask or observe what your partner likes when they're out dining at a restaurant or what they grab from a grocery run. See how often they get sweets for themselves. Is it a regular treat that they eat or do they only get something if it's a special occasion?

If there are days when your partner is in need of a pick me up, take a trip to their favorite shop or restaurant to get them their favorite dessert. Surprise them if they've expressed that they aren't having a great day or had a tough day at work. Use the sweet as a way to get them into a better mood or work out a way to get them to talk about what their day was like. Give it to them after their last meal to make it a bit more special and something that they're able to look forward to after a taxing day.

The reasons for getting your partner's favorite treat don't have to be just for comfort. You can get them their favorite when they get a promotion at work or finish a tough project. You can make it something you do regularly, maybe an every month or every few weeks tradition when you have a little cash to spare. Don't be afraid to be spontaneous either; you could be just passing by a restaurant with the cheesecake that your partner loves while coming home from an errand and pick up a slice for them then.

If you really want to go above and beyond for your lover's sweet tooth, learn how to make a copycat recipe of their favorite treat. This way, you won't need to travel to get their favorite cake or cookie, you'll be able to make it yourself! This would be especially great for their birthday, letting you make the full dessert without limiting them to just getting a piece or two. Sure, it might not be the same as their favorite, but it may become something they look forward to you making for them on special occasions. Let the sweets your partner loves help to form just as sweet memories between the two of you as you go through life together.

Chapter 41
Let's Hear It for the Boy (or Girl)

W e're in everyone's business nowadays. Social media is the best place to find out what's going on in other people's lives and see how the people you're friends with are doing. Posting photos, status updates, and just general news on social media is the norm now and I'm sure that you've got an account somewhere that you're using for those reasons too. However, in order to make sure that your lover is getting their fair share of attention on those sites, you'll need to first make sure that it's okay with them if you post things about what they're doing and any updates in their life. If your partner wishes to keep certain things private, respect that decision.

For the things that they are willing to share, get some posts out about your partner! Tag them and congratulate them on a promotion or graduating from school. Put up statuses to show what you and your lover are doing over the weekend or just post about how much you love them. Friends and family will gush and congratulate them based on your post and maybe help give them something nice to read after a grueling day.

Always check with your partner about posting specific things. If you and your partner are expecting, but they don't want to share the news yet, respect their decision. Compromise on posting about announcements that'll take place in a few week's time in order to get your audience's anticipation going. Let your friends and family know about something that your partner is working up towards, getting them to send messages of encouragement and luck to your partner to help them get pumped up. Use your social media as a place to boost your love and affection for your partner and let others join in to give their own words of affirmation to them.

Chapter 42
How Do I Love Thee?

Sometimes, one of the best ways to let your partner know how much you love them is to tell them. Whether it's through a conversation, a call, a text, or a note, making sure that your partner knows how much you appreciate and love them is as simple as those three little words: I love you. Of course, I'm sure that you'd love to express that sentiment with more than three words, so here's a little something I think both you and your partner will love.

Get a greeting card and fill it with as many things as you can about what you love about your partner. Spare no detail, write as much as you can to fill up any empty space. Then, take that card and send it through the mail addressed to your lover. It'll come to your address in a few days and don't act too suspicious if your partner asks about it. Let them read it to themselves and let them know if you ran out of space to keep telling them how much you love them. Let the rest of your time go from there, whether it leads to something a bit steamy is completely up to you.

You can also keep a journal to write your love story down in. When you and your lover aren't at your best, you can open up this journal to read about just what made you two fall in love in the first place. Have your lover add things about you that they love and document your feelings if you're having a fight. Learn from the journaled thoughts and ideas to better understand each other when talking isn't something you want to do. Let these thoughts remind you that love has its ups and downs and that even during a fight, that love you have for each other is still there.

Sugar, this means that you're going to have to be very open about your feelings. Let everything out onto the pages of your journal. Don't think about your lover reading your thoughts, let them get written out unimpeded. Journaling can help you come to terms on certain issues you and your partner might disagree about or help bring shape to your feelings on something that you're having trouble expressing through speech. Openness and communication is key to any successful relationship, so make sure that you provide the same opportunity to your partner if they need time to get their thoughts and feelings out on a page.

Chapter 43
Lunch on Me

Your partner can sometimes be in need of a little extra care, if they're experiencing a lot of stress at work or somewhere else outside of the house. It can get overwhelming for them that, at some point, they might forget to do simple things like pack lunch or remember an appointment. Sticky note reminders are a helpful way to make sure they remember, but what about if they're gone for the day and don't have their lunch?

You can surprise your lover, once you realize they don't have anything to eat or they left their packed lunch in your fridge, by ordering from an app and having their favorite fast food meal delivered to their place of work. Many apps can have you send meals as a gift, so you can make sure that it's being delivered to the correct person. It doesn't have to be a secret for your lover to know who it's from, but it could be fun to pretend like you didn't do anything when they get home and ask you about it. A little teasing will show them that what you did may not have seemed like a huge deal, but knowing that you did it will make sure they know you're watching out for them.

If your lover usually packs a lunch, switch out their creation for one that you made. You can fill their pack with the foods that they enjoy or something that they didn't have time to make because of their schedule. Add a little note along with their meal to make sure they know you're thinking about them during work and that you hope they have a good day.

If you have a day off and your partner doesn't, let them know that you'll stop by to deliver their lunch. Even during a hectic workday, your lover being able to see you for a few minutes and then taking time to eat something that you prepared (or at least hand delivered to them) will make their day much nicer. You don't have to be physically with your partner to make sure that they're being taken care of, so consider these lunches as a way to show you're aware of how they're doing and you want to help however you can.

Chapter 44
Say It with Flowers

I 'll say something that many people might find a bit dramatic: I don't care who you are, but everyone likes to get flowers or plants as a gift. I don't care if you're masculine, feminine, neither, or both, having someone give you a living thing that smells good is always appreciated. It doesn't have to be a huge bouquet of flowers or a decorative plant, even just something small can bring a smile to your lover's face.

First and foremost, you'll need to make sure that your partner doesn't have any specific allergies to certain plants or pollen. This could have a gift of flowers turning into a day of sneezing or, in extreme cases, a trip to the hospital. Find out what they prefer in terms of flowers. Do they like a specific color of flowers? If they're not good with pollen, what's another plant that they like to be around? Would they rather have something that smells good than looks good? If not a flower, would a succulent or herb be a better fit? Keep these thoughts in mind when choosing a plant to give them.

If you want a bit more flair to your gift, have it delivered to your partner's workplace. A courier or a member of staff will need to have it delivered, so it'll be a welcome surprise if your partner's having a rough day. Seeing a bouquet of flowers or a pretty plant being placed on their desk with a card from you will probably be a highlight of their day and give them a needed moment to relax and admire what you gave them. If they're allowed to keep plants or flowers at their workspace, it can be a great reminder of your love for them whenever they come in for the day, a reason for them to take a moment to smile and know that they are loved.

If you'd rather give your lover flowers or plants at home, make sure that you're getting the most out of their freshness. Flowers should be placed into water, if not planted in soil, and have that water refreshed every day. For the first few days, add some sugar to the water to keep the petals looking vibrant. They'll eventually need to be removed, since dying flowers can bring those pesky little flies into your home, but you can always replace them, especially if your partner lets you know that they enjoyed the gesture.

For plants, make sure that you're putting it in a pot with good drainage that isn't too small for the plant. Water your plant as needed in order to keep it green and growing for weeks to come. Another option is, after the plants or flowers get too large in their pots, you can plant them outside and let nature do the watering. Having something that is constantly growing and can potentially come back for years to come can be a great addition to your home and be a reminder of just how much the love between you and your partner has grown.

Chapter 45
Putty in Your Hands

We've gone over how a couple's massage can be a great way for you and your partner to relax. Massages help to ease tension and get someone feeling calmer and relaxed with just some practiced touches. You don't have to have massages as a couple to feel that type of relaxation, so what's stopping you from becoming a masseuse for your partner?

You might need to do a little research, just to make sure that you're massaging the right places to give your partner a good massage. Some of the easiest massages can be done to the feet and legs, so if you're not used to giving one, start there. If you're a bit unsure as to how to begin broaching the subject of massaging your partner, work it into a full day of pampering when they've got time off. Create a whole day around the spa experience, complete with aromatherapy candles, a freshly drawn bath, fluffy towels, and 'complimentary' drinks.

Once your partner is out of their bath and feeling cozy, start your massage. Use lightly or unscented oils to rub into their skin to keep it feeling soft and lock in the moisture from their bath. Don't use too much or you'll end with stained furniture and sheets; only use enough that, when massaging it into your partner's skin, there isn't a shiny residue left over. Work on whatever part of their body you're comfortable with or give them a full body massage if you're a pro.

Have your partner tell you if anything makes them uncomfortable or hurts. The experience is supposed to be a pleasurable one, so if you're massaging onto a raw nerve or muscle, that's not good. Take your time and don't rush; appreciate your partner's body and what work they put into it that's making it sore. Let them know that they deserve to have a break from that work and that you're more than happy to give them the relief they need.

And, of course, what massage isn't complete without a happy ending? Just make sure that your partner's in the mood for it so that all of your hard work in getting them to relax isn't for nothing. No one likes something like that to be sprung on them when you're ready for a nap.

Chapter 46
How Do You Like Your Eggs?

W e've gone over the importance of meals that you create with and for your partner and how much it means to them giving them something nourishing they can use to get through their day. Why not start with the most important meal of the day and make sure that your partner doesn't have to lift a finger for it?

Breakfast in bed is one of the best things that you can surprise your lover with. My partner will make it for me the day after I've had a rough time or for a special occasion, but you can make your partner breakfast in bed whenever you want to. If your partner's a light sleeper, make sure you let them know that you're just going to do some chores so that they don't get suspicious about the noises they hear. I'm a bit clumsy in the kitchen myself, but I don't have to worry about that because my partner could sleep through a hurricane.

Plan out in advance what you want to make, just so you're not scrambling for ingredients and making more noise for your partner to get worried about. Set things aside so that they're easy to grab or pre-make batter or dough the day before so all you'll need to do is cook or defrost your food. Especially if you want to make something a little more complicated for your lover, preparation is key and will be paramount in showing your lover just how much thought you put into the meal.

Make your lover's favorites for their breakfast in bed. Make sure you're not overloading them with the amount of food you're making, just so they're able to enjoy it and not feel sick if they've eaten too much. If you want to make it a bit more romantic, you can feed them the first few bites yourself. You can join them once you've served them and spend the morning reclining as you eat.

If there are leftovers, perfect! Did you know that pancakes and waffles freeze pretty well? Can't say the same for eggs or other additions to your breakfast in bed, but if you've found you've made a bit too much for the both of you to finish up, then you can save the leftovers for another day. I've found that having breakfast for dinner, even when it's not in bed, is a fun way to turn around expectations if you'd want to try something a bit different for your last meal of the day.

Chapter 47
In Sickness and In Health

G etting sick is never fun. Regardless if you have a small cold or the flu, sometimes an illness can knock you down for the count and all you can think about doing is curling up in bed until it passes. Being with your lover will tune you into how they're feeling and if they're under the weather, even if they don't want to show it. If you notice that your lover isn't feeling their best, it's time to step up.

Take charge when your partner is feeling ill and make sure that any errands or chores that they'd usually perform are done. Go out to the store and grab any medication that they need in order to feel better. Get nutritious food to help get their strength up or bland food if their stomach is bothering them. Don't let them worry about anything and be the one who takes care of them, showing them that you're perfectly capable of doing things by yourself.

The goal of your behavior is to let your partner know that you're more than happy to take care of them when they're ill and can manage things on your own if something were to happen to them. However, understand that them being sick might make them feel vulnerable and like you didn't need them for anything. Use this time to reassure them that just because they're not able to help you now doesn't mean that you don't appreciate their help when they're not sick.

That said, don't try and push yourself too hard either. Don't overload your plate with everything that you're responsible for, along with all of the tasks that your partner usually completes. Work to keep things manageable; you are just one person after all. The last thing you need is to get sick as well from doing too much and, let me tell you, it's worse when you and your lover are both sick and trying to get each other better. I can remember one time that my husband and I both came down with a sinus infection the same week. Had us bullying each other to run out to the store to get medicine, even when just the breeze on our noses was enough to trigger one of the worst headaches I ever had.

Chapter 48
How Do I Look?

H unny, one of the few things that your lover knows about you is what you're comfortable with wearing. If they're attentive, they might know that you like to change out of your work clothes and into something comfy. They might know that you prefer matching PJs or an oversized t-shirt to wear to bed. Or that your idea of dressing up is wearing something other than sweatpants. I'm sure you know the same types of things about your lover too, even if you don't realize it.

If your lover is one for fashion, or at least knows what you like to wear, they've probably bought you a few things for your wardrobe. The articles of clothing might not be something that you're wearing every single day, but they're probably still hanging somewhere in your closet, just waiting for an opportunity to be put on. What I want you to do is find something in your wardrobe that your partner picked out for you. Maybe they did it because the color matches your eyes. Maybe it was something they wanted to have you wear just for them. Maybe they thought it'd make you look very, very good, so much so that they'd want to peel that outfit off whenever you wore it. Grab it and, when you and your partner are alone, put it on and see what they think.

If your partner's given you lots of clothing, you can make something of a fashion show during a day when you both are home. Get changed into various outfits throughout the day and watch as your partner looks you up and down with a smile on their face. As for what happens next, that all depends on you and your partner.

I can't help but think of a time I did something similar. My husband had gotten me a lovely emerald dress. I thought it was a tad too revealing to wear out to dinner, but he'd gotten it because the color reminded him of my eyes. He thought it'd look good on me and, even if I didn't wear it out, he wanted to see me try it on. I did, got myself all gussied up like I was going out for a night on the town, then headed into the living room to show him. I have to admit, he was right about the color; it was gorgeous and didn't make me look washed out like some of the darker colors of clothing tend to do. My husband was very, very happy that I gave it a shot and...well, I'm sure you can imagine how the night went.

Chapter 49
For Your Eyes Only

K eeping on the topic of clothing, the appeal of having something underneath your clothing that has you feeling some type of way can boost anyone's confidence while also making them more than ready to head back home to give their lover a view of what they're wearing. Lingerie seems to have always been something that couples will buy each other for romantic occasions, whether to have their lover be surprised when stripping them down or for you and your lover to change into before things get a bit...hot. I'll try and keep things as above board as I can, sugar, but no promises.

Get some lingerie or sleepwear for your lover that you know they'll enjoy. Check what their tastes are, keep their favorite colors and fabrics in mind, and choose something that you know they'll feel great wearing. It doesn't need to be a special occasion for you to pick out something for them. Pick a time when they're having a rough go of it or if they've had a slew of bad days at work. Use something they're celebrating as an excuse, but go all out to find something that you know for a fact that they'll love.

Check with them about certain things that make them feel their best or a bit saucy when they wear them. Maybe they're the type of person that takes comfort above all else? Or they could be someone that will put every single snap and clip into place, even if all of their hard work will be undone once you get your hands on them. Observe if there was something specific they'd been looking at while you were out clothing shopping or if they mentioned something about a certain style that the store you were at didn't have. You'll need to pay attention to some of these details, especially if you're looking to surprise your partner, but don't be afraid to ask if you're not sure if they'd like something specific.

This can also be an opportunity to push your partner's boundaries. Again, and I'll keep saying this until I'm blue in the face, talk to your partner to see what they're comfortable with and what are things that they absolutely will not go for. Who knows, they might just surprise you.

Now, for the reveal. Plan a night with your lover that you'll use to present their new lingerie or sleepwear. Have them take their time changing, keeping the anticipation going until they come out to reveal themselves. After that, well, you two can get as saucy as you'd like. Make sure to compliment your lover on how they look, all dressed up in something you got especially for them. How the color or the style suits them and hugs them in all the right places. How seeing them looking so nice, just for you, is worth taking everything off so that you can show them just what a gorgeous person they are.

Is it getting steamy in here again? Whoo, give me a few, sugar, I've got to take some time away for a spell.

Chapter 50
The Soundtrack to Our Romance

I'm sure that there are songs that you and your lover are fond of. Maybe there's an artist that the two of you bonded over when you first started dating or a song that brings back a memory of when you shared your first kiss. As you two have continued your relationship, you probably have a whole list of songs that you can associate with different moments that the two of you shared or songs that describe some of the aspects of how you feel when you're together.

Take some time to come up with a custom playlist or two for your lover that includes songs the two of you enjoy or that have a special meaning for you. You can create multiple lists that might be themed around specific parts of your life. Your lover might have songs that they like to do chores to that gets them pumped and ready to get your place clean. You could make a playlist of songs that you two love to sing along with in the car, regardless if you're apart from each other or together. If you've taking dancing classes, find the songs that you and your partner dance the best to or find the songs that are your go-tos for when you're out and want to do karaoke. Whatever those songs are or however many kinds of lists you can think of, bring them together and have the playlist completed for your partner to listen to.

If you're using an app or website, sometimes there are descriptions that you can give your playlists to help them stand out. Once you've decided on a list or two that you want to create, make a little note in the description of the playlist to let your lover know how much these songs mean to you and what sort of memories they evoke. Present the list to them as something they can listen to in the car or while they're at work. Once they listen to it, see how they liked it. Take their suggestions for new songs to add or if they remind you of a song that would be great with what you already have.

One thing that I think needs to be said is that if you can't come up with multiple lists, that's fine. Create a playlist of the songs that you and your partner share a memory with or a love for. This doesn't have to be a complex declaration of how much you care for them, just a simple way for them to turn on some music and be reminded of you. If you want, this can be something that the two of you collaborate to create. Work with each other to make something that you can both listen to and think fondly of your lover as you go about your day.

Epilogue

Well, I think that just about does it. A nice group of fifty ways to keep your lover.

As I mentioned before, these are suggestions and can be tweaked to fit your situation or taste. I don't know what you and your lover are able to do or not do, so nothing in this book is set in stone as the end-all-be-all. Rework aspects to help keep things flexible. The main goal is to create something with your lover that you two can share, whether it be just a memory of a moment in time, the recipe for your new favorite meal, or a list of songs that gets you both singing out loud. Again, I'm not an expert, but I'd bet that at least one of these suggestions will be a wonderful way to connect with your lover.

Remember, hunny, that at the heart of every successful relationship lies a commitment to open communication, a deep sense of intimacy, and unwavering trust. The steps outlined in this book are not just about grand gestures but about building and reinforcing these critical aspects every day. Talk to your partner about your feelings, create intimate moments that are just for the two of you, and always strive to be trustworthy in your actions. By doing so, you're not just following a guide—you're laying down the very foundation of a love that can withstand the test of time.

I'm sure I took a few detours here and there, but hopefully not too many that had you lose interest or forget what you were reading. I appreciate that Anissa made sure that I didn't get into anything too saucy for you all to be reading about. Again, I'm a proper Southern woman that won't take this book being about just the saucy things that can spice up a relationship. The last thing you need is someone looking over your shoulder and thinking you'd picked up something a bit spicier than your average book.

What I hope that you, dear reader, have learned from this is that there are so many ways to show your love for your partner. Each of the points I've made is just a facet of your relationship that you can work to polish into something that gleams bright enough that the rest of the world can see it without you and your lover even saying a word. Will that gleam be something that appears in an instant? Probably not. These steps aren't a cure-all for the times when you and your lover are having a rough patch; they're merely here to show that there are so many different ways that you can appreciate your lover and what they've given you in your relationship.

And, who knows? There could be more than fifty ways to keep your lover...

Belle Wether

Afterword

I n the Introduction of this book, you were introduced to the Intimacy Growth Framework, a tailored approach designed to help you and your lover grow closer over time. This framework isn't just about big gestures or grand acts; it's about the small, everyday moments that, when nurtured, blossom into deeper connections. The beauty of the Intimacy Growth Framework is that it's flexible—just like the suggestions in this book. You and your partner can decide how to incorporate these ideas into your lives, whether it's by trying out one new activity each month or sprinkling smaller gestures throughout your week.

What this framework offers is a structured yet adaptable way to build intimacy. By focusing on emotional, mental, and physical connections, it guides you to strengthen your bond in meaningful ways. And while there's no magic formula for love, this framework gives you the tools to create a lasting, profound relationship.

Let these steps, guided by the Intimacy Growth Framework, be ways that you can deepen what you already have with your lover. Give them time, plan, and communicate with your lover about how you want things to work, and you won't be disappointed. Let them help you both see different aspects of yourselves that you might not have normally seen. Take those chances, no matter how little they appear. Learn a new skill. Try a new dish. Find what makes your lover comfortable in a way you didn't realize was possible. With your commitment and effort, you can truly design the relationship of your dreams.

Appendix

Step into the enchanting realm of Belle Wether Romance, where love blooms and relationships thrive. This captivating book is just the beginning of a journey filled with heartfelt advice, thoughtful insights, and a touch of Southern charm.

With Belle Wether Romance, you'll discover more than just a book. It's an invitation to cultivate and nurture your relationships, creating lasting bonds that stand the test of time. Alongside this treasure trove of wisdom, you'll soon find an array of helpful publications and tools designed to support you every step of the way.

Imagine documenting your own love story in the pages of our beautifully crafted journals and scrapbooks, which are set to launch soon. These cherished keepsakes will serve as a testament to your journey, capturing cherished memories and treasured moments along the way. Keep an eye out for these journals, as they will be the first in a series of products aimed at helping you create and preserve the magic of your relationship.

Soon, you'll be able to download the Belle Wether Romance Mobile App, designed to help you stay on top of your relationship goals. With this app, you'll never let too much time pass without showing your love and appreciation. Say goodbye to forgetfulness and hello to heartfelt gestures that will keep the flame of romance burning bright.

And let's not forget about the delicious side of romance. Our collection of cookbooks, coming soon, will empower you to create culinary masterpieces for your loved ones. From delectable desserts that melt hearts to savory dishes that ignite taste buds, these recipes are sure to add an extra sprinkle of love to every meal shared together.

For those looking to deepen their connection and enhance their relationship skills, Belle Wether Romance will soon offer an array of online courses that guide you through the Intimacy Growth Framework. These courses are designed to provide you with practical tools and techniques that can be immediately applied to your relationship. Whether you're just starting out or looking to rekindle the spark, our courses will cater to every stage of love, helping you build a foundation of trust, communication, and intimacy.

Additionally, we invite you to join our exclusive online community membership site, launching soon. Here, you'll connect with like-minded individuals who are also on a journey to strengthen their relationships. This supportive space will offer members access to expert advice, interactive workshops, and a wealth of resources that will inspire you to nurture and grow your love. Together, we'll explore new ways to deepen your bond, ensuring that your relationship continues to blossom.

So why wait? Embrace the magic of Belle Wether Romance and embark on a journey towards deeper connections, meaningful conversations, and a love that blossoms like never before. Let this collection of soon-to-be-available books and tools be your trusted companions as you create your very own love story – one page at a time.

Stay up-to-date on the availability of the Belle Wether Romance collection on belle-wether.com or follow us on social media @BelleWetherRomance.

Bibliography

Sources:

- Bowlby, J. (1988). *A Secure Base: Parent-Child Attachment and Healthy Human Development*. Basic Books.

- Chapman, G. (1992). *The Five Love Languages: How to Express Heartfelt Commitment to Your Mate*. Northfield Publishing.

- Goleman, D. (1995). *Emotional Intelligence: Why It Can Matter More Than IQ*. Bantam Books.

- Gottman, J. M., & Silver, N. (1999). *The Seven Principles for Making Marriage Work*. Harmony Books.

- Gottman Institute. (2020). *The Science of Couples and Family Therapy: Behind the Scenes at the "Love Lab"*. Retrieved from Gottman Institute

- Fiese, B. H. (2007). *Family Routines and Rituals*. Yale University Press.

- Carroll, L. (2013). *Mindfulness-Based Relationship En-*

hancement: Theoretical Foundations and Empirical Support.

- ChatGPT, OpenAI's language model, contributed to the synthesis and articulation of the Intimacy Growth Framework™ based on these sources and additional contextual analysis.